MW00652704

MARCO CRESCENZI

The SILVER BEATLES

MARCO CRESCENZI

The SILVER BEATLES

A Story of Struggle, Luck and Genius:
the Beatles before they
became the Beatles

EDITION OLMS ZÜRICH

First English Language Edition 2024
Copyright © Edition Olms AG, Zürich

Edition Olms AG
Rosengartenstr. 13B
CH-8608 Bubikon/Zürich

Mail: info@edition-olms.com
Web: www.edition-olms.com

ISBN 978-3-283-01332-5

Bibliographic information from the Deutsche Nationalbibliothek
The Deutsche Nationalbibliothek lists this publication in the Deutsche Nationalbibliografie;
detailed bibliographic data are available on the Internet at http://dnb.d-nb.de.

All rights reserved.
No part in this publication may be reproduced, stored in a retrieval system or transmitted in any form or
by any means, electronic, mechanical, photocopying, recording or otherwise, without the permission of
the copyright holder.

COVER AND DESIGN: Francesco Partesano

FRONT COVER: The first Beatles promotion card.
From left: John Lennon, George Harrison, Paul McCartney, and Pete Best.

BACK COVER: George Harrison, John Lennon, and Paul McCartney.

PHOTO CREDITS: Brian Epstein photo p. 52: Joop van Bilsen (Collectie/ Archief: Fotocollectie Anefo/
Wikimedia Commons). Photo pp. 162-163: West Midlands Police/Wikipedia Commons. Photo on p. 164:
Noord-Hollands Archief/Fotoburo de Boer/Wikimedia Commons e Collectie/Archief: Fotocollectie
Anefo/Wikimedia Commons. All other photos are from the Author's personal archives. Please note
that although the Publisher has made all efforts to trace photographers' names for due credit, some
searches were to no avail. The Publisher apologizes for any omissions, and agrees to make any revisions
to credits in the event there are reprints of this book.

First published in Italian Edition by
GREMESE EDITORE
2005/2022 c E.G.E. s.r.l. – Rome

PRINTED IN LITHUANIA

Contents

Preface

There have been rivers of words of course written about John Winston Lennon, James Paul McCartney, George Harrison, and Richard Starkey (stage name Ringo Starr). "The Beatles" are a universal phenomenon.

Yet perhaps little or nothing is known about such names as Stuart Sutcliffe, Pete Best, Pete Shotton, Rodney Davis, Eric Griffiths, Colin Hanton, Len Garry, Ivan Vaughan, Nigel Whalley, Bill Smith, John "Duff" Lowe, or Kenneth Brown. They were part of a succession of musicians who came and went during the early days of the band. Some were well-known and others not at all, but all of them at one time had a place beside the four lads from Liverpool.

The period we are talking about began in the mid-fifties. It continued until the turning point date of Friday, 5 October 1962. That was when Parlophone released the Beatles' first single, catalogue number R4949 (Side A: *Love Me Do*; Side B: *P.S. I Love You*). This was not just any record of the many releases of those years. Indeed it had the power to change the course of the history of music and even more...

The protagonists of this story are many, really so many. We will be helped by the words and images from those times, from 1956 to the year 1963. That latter year set the seal on the Beatles' success forever.

We will follow the thread that leads from the Quarrymen (or was it Quarry Men?) to The Beatles, by way of "Long John and the Silver Beatles", the "Beatals", the "Silver Beetles", "Johnny & the Moondogs", and even the "Nerk Twins", just to mention a few of the incarnations of the Liverpool band.

We will try to find our way through those tumultuous times using the countless photos from the Author's personal collection and the many finds from his research. They will take us back to that 'heroic' period to relive all of the exploits and struggles of the entangled roots of the Beatles... before they became "The Beatles!"

Marco Crescenzi

1956 – 1959

In the beginning there was skiffle

What in the world could have occurred in the year of our Lord 1956 in a city like Liverpool (quite frankly in those days not a terribly exciting city) that suddenly got the bored local youth buzzing? As strange as it may seem, all it took was for an absolutely impossible character (at least that was his image) like Lonnie Donegan to have recorded a song two years before that, in July 1954, in the States. The song was *Rock Island Line*, and in January 1956, it took everyone by surprise and became a tremendous hit in Britain.

Hundreds, in fact thousands of kids, suddenly grabbed whatever produced a sound and started to… make music! Yes, because ladies and gentlemen, here came the birth of *Skiffle*. Or rather, this was when the U.K. suddenly discovered something called skiffle actually existed. It was a music genre that actually originated in the United States, and had been played there since the end of the 1920s by the descendants of the African people taken into slavery.

Only rarely did they have access to musical instruments, and so to make music they invented their own. They created instruments from found objects and anything that made a sound, whether a washboard, discarded lead pipe, or even a busted guitar that could be patched up.

What was really great was that to play skiffle you needed no particular training. You did not even have to know how to read music! Thousands of amateurs took the plunge as a result of this brilliant discovery. Among them we see a certain John Winston Lennon, at the time struggling furiously with a

A fourteen-year-old
Paul McCartney on the porch
trying out his guitar
guaranteed "unbreakable".

**22 June 1957, Rosebery Street.
The Quarrymen perform
on the trailer of a truck used for
transporting coal. On the bass drum
the logo of the band with
the original graphics: "Quarry Men".**

horrible guitar from which he could not produce a sound.

And then, among the thousands of young fans waiting for an autograph outside the stage door of Liverpool's Empire Theatre – where the messiah of the new skiffle religion, the previously mentioned Lonnie Donegan, had just wrapped up his show – we find a fourteen-year-old James Paul McCartney. At the time, he was a little better than Lennon on the guitar, but still not really up to par either. At this point the two do not know each other, so let us leave Paul as he waits determined to get his autograph, and continue our story with John.

John belonged to the ranks of baby boomers in England. This was the generation that had been born during WWII and had grown up during the period right after the war, with all of its hardships. By 1956, John was already a streetwise toughie and leader of his own neighbourhood gang. And of course he wanted to take up the national craze of skiffle too. The fact that he did not have the slightest notion of how to play any musical instrument whatsoever seemed irrelevant.

John got right to work recruiting some of his classmates and buddies. They would form a skiffle band, one of the thousands in England at the time elbowing their way to perform on stage.

Mark Lewisohn, an authority considered the greatest "Beatles egghead" of all time, in his book *The Complete Beatles Chronicle*, sets the date of John Lennon's stage debut as 9 June 1957. What is certain is that the five (yes, after many ups and downs, the band finally settled on five musicians: John Lennon as "supreme commander", his close friend Pete Shotton, Bill Smith, Ivan Vaughan and Nigel Whalley), performed in a few undocumented performances in 1956. These were followed by appearances during March and April 1957 at venues in Liverpool that we are more certain about. There were places like the Grafton Ballroom, Locarno Ballroom, Pavilion Theatre and Rialto Ballroom. In March 1957 the duo John Lennon and Pete Shotton appeared in a place called the Black Jacks.

These were mysterious, nebulous events that even today seem suspended somewhere between myth and reality. Actually quite a few years later, the original members of the Quarrymen (Pete Shotten, Eric Griffiths, Colin Hanton and Ivan Vaughan) were asked to recall that distant past. Those were the days when the band yearned for the chance to play at a church fete or other such gig. Their memories, however, were by then too fuzzy to be of much help.

This brings us to the famous date of 9 June 1957. The Quarrymen performed at the Empire Theatre that day in a competitive audition for the Carrol Levis TV show "Search for the Stars" (Lewisohn claims the program was called "TV Star Search"). The Quarrymen, however, lost to the unknown Sunnyside Skiffle Group. After that experience, a first change in the band's lineup ensued...

The date of 22 June 1957 marked the first appearance of the Quarrymen to be documented by photos. This was on the occasion of the 750th Anniversary of the Concession by King John of the Letters Patent (known as the Royal Charter) to the colonists who founded Liverpool.

In keeping with the band's name ('Quarrymen' not only referred to the name Quarry Bank High School, but also literally referred to "men from the quarry" or miners), the boys performed on a coal wagon.

Chronicles from the time relate how it was all organized by Mrs. Marjorie Roberts and her son Charles, a friend of Collin Hanton's (the band's drummer). Charles invited the band to perform and even drew their logo on the bass drum. The "cooperative" of Rosebery Street residents supplied the coal wagon and electricity for the instruments (the gentleman who lived at 76 let them pass the cable through his window). At the end of the concert, Mrs. Roberts was even able to come to their rescue by offering the band a refuge when a neighbourhood gang found John Lennon a little too bossy.

Thanks to this strategic retreat, the five musicians could hide out in the

Poster of the parish church fete in Woolton. The Quarrymen are officially presented as a "skiffle group".

Roberts' living room and, after tea and biscuits, return home safe and sound. Charles Roberts and his mother made a historic contribution to music history by taking photos of the Quarrymen during that show.

Based on the rather blurry accounts later of those who were present, the songs the band played during the two performances (afternoon and evening) could have been:

Twenty Flight Rock
Be-Bop-A-Lula
Cumberland Gap
Maggie Mae
Railroad Bill
Come Go with Me
Hound Dog!
Blue Suede Shoes

**6 July 1957. St. Peter's Church fete.
John Lennon (centre in a light checked shirt)
just before meeting Paul McCartney.**

The members of the band were:

Colin Hanton	—	Drums
Eric Griffiths	—	Guitar
John Lennon	—	Voice/Guitar
Ivan Vaughan	—	Bass/Tea Chest
Pete Shotton	—	Washboard

Congratulations Quarrymen, you have just stepped into the dazzling world of show biz. Now though, it was time to get serious. Destiny offered help when from 3:00 pm on 6 July 1957, the Quarrymen were asked to give two performances at the local St. Peter's Church fete. Now, you might think, not a big deal. But this was not exactly true, since addition to being the band's second performance documented by photos, it was also...

...The day Paul met John

The Quarrymen gave two shows that day, the first in the afternoon on the lawn behind the church, where they played on a wobbly makeshift stage, and the second in the evening, in one of the rooms inside the church building.

During the afternoon show, a fifteen-year-old Paul McCartney met a tipsy John Lennon who was just going on seventeen at the time. The latter was singing at the top of his lungs, making up lyrics to *Go with Me*. In keeping with the tremendously self-satisfied image that still pursues Paul today, at the end of the concert he immediately seized the occasion to show Lennon how ignorant he was of music. McCartney played an absolutely flawless *Twenty Flight Rock* on the spot and then transcribed the exact lyrics of *Be-Bop-A-Lula* for John.

**Paul McCartney, John Lennon and George
Harrison perform without a drummer
at the wedding of George's brother.**

Lennon was so impressed that a little later he sent his squire, Pete Shotton, to McCartney's to invite him to join the band. Paul said he would "think about it"... Paul's debut with the Quarrymen only occurred on 18 October 1957, when the band played at the New Clubmoor Hall (Conservative Party's club) of Liverpool.

The only details with proof about the historic day that John and Paul met (6 July 1957) are the songs the Quarrymen played which were:

Be-Bop-A-Lula
Cumberland Gap
Maggie Mae
Railroad Bill
Come Go with Me

The members of the band were: :

Afternoon Concert
Colin Hanton   –   Drums
Eric Griffiths   –   Guitar
John Lennon   –   Voice / Guitar
Ivan Vaughan   –   Bass / Tea Chest
Pete Shotton   –   Washboard

Evening Concert
Eric Griffiths   –   Guitar
John Lennon   –   Voice / Guitar
Ivan Vaughan   –   Bass / Tea Chest
Pete Shotton   –   Washboard
(Colin Hanton was absent and the drummer from the George Edward's Band replaced him.)

Just think – we have now witnessed the historic encounter between two of the world's greatest music legends. Not bad for a start...

The adventures of our heroes continue and lead us to two appearances, one during July 1957 at Quarry Bank High School, and another on 7 August at the Cavern Club. Yes! For all of you Beatles eggheads this is *the* Cavern Club! That night on the bill there were also the Darktown Skittle Group, the Deltones and the Demon Five.

Our heroes, without Paul McCartney yet (he was busy with the Scouts, or so the official version goes) played three songs: *Come Go with Me*, *Hound Dog* and *Blue Suede Shoes*. That is, before they were booed off the stage for having broken the unwritten golden rule of "no rock 'n' roll, only skiffle".

And so this brings us to the fateful evening of 18 October 1957, to the show at the New Clubmoor Hall of Liverpool. That night Paul McCartney joined John Lennon onstage with the Quarrymen for the first time. After a performance in a bus depot and another in a slaughterhouse (or maybe its recreation centre) we come to 23 November 1957.

This was when the "dynamic duo" Lennon and McCartney were immortalized for the first time in photos. It was the band's second performance at the Norris

23 November 1957.
New Clubmoor Hall.
Paul and John, in waiters' jackets,
perform as duo leaders of
the Quarrymen.

Green Conservative Party club. The only difference of note – other than the waiters' jackets that John and Paul decided to wear as leaders of the group – was a change in lineup which was:

Colin Hanton — Drums
Eric Griffiths — Guitar
John Lennon — Voice / Guitar
Len Garry — Bass / Tea Chest
Paul McCartney — Voice / Guitar

Two musicians had been "purged" from the Quarrymen, Ivan Vaughan and Pete Shotton.

Life was a struggle for an emerging band. The Quarrymen, with the Lennon-McCartney duo at its helm, persevered in fits and starts. As we follow the timeline

George Harrison, John Lennon
and Paul McCartney during
a performance at a private party.

set by the photos, we come to a tumultuous period in the band's history with several lineup changes.

During this time an event of note occurred that involved the Beatles and a record. Indeed, the authoritative British collectors' monthly *Record Collector* deemed this Beatles disc to be no less than "the rarest record in the world".

It all began in 1955 at the height of the skiffle craze with its dozens and dozens of bands eager to record their own material. Percy Phillips, the owner of an electricity shop in Liverpool, spent the rather substantial sum of 400£ to buy a tape recorder, a record pressing machine, a 4-track mixer and some microphones. He set it all up in the living room of the family home in Liverpool, at 38 Kensington.

Phillip's idea was to round up the bands in the area and, for a fee, offer to make records and tapes for them in his "recording studio". The musicians could come to the house by tram (it conveniently passed by the Phillips' house).

They would perform their songs while Phillips, set up in the kitchen, would tape record them. A machine transferred the recording onto an acetate disc which the customer would be given. The tape, of course, was rewound and used again to record the next band. Unless, as we will see, the band had enough money to pay the extra charge to buy it.

Phillips soon became very popular among the Liverpool skiffle bands. Our quintet, the Quarrymen, of course was no exception. The members of their band were now John Lennon, Paul McCartney and George Harrison (guitar), John Lowe (piano), and Colin Hanton (drums).

Sometime between the spring and summer of 1958 they went to Phillips' to "make a record" as they said in those days. (Lewisohn in his *Chronicle* dates this event to sometime in mid-1958, whereas Hunter Davies in *The Quarrymen* claims it was towards the end of that year).

For 17 schillings and 6d (about 18 £ today, or 21 $, if you prefer), the Quarrymen left the house with their precious, very fragile 10" 78 rpm, but without the tape, which they could not afford. The label on the record did not mention the name Quarrymen, nor of course the Beatles, since the latter name was only adopted a couple of years later.

On one side there was a tribute to Buddy Holly, *That'll Be the Day*, and on the other, a song by McCartney-Harrison, *In Spite of All the Danger*. John Lennon was leading solo voice on both songs.

In 1981 John Lowe owned the only copy of this record. He decided to sell it at a Sotheby's auction where its worth was estimated at approximately £5000. McCartney obtained a court order to block the sale and, in the highhanded way it was thought typical of him, he tried to force Lowe to give him the record. Paul had no real legal footing to claim the disc and so the good McCartney was "obliged" to buy it for an undisclosed amount. (This inconsolably pained him beyond words). As for Lowe, he was obliged to sign a statement agreeing not to reveal the amount he had received.

The "rarest record in the world", the 78 rpm of *That'll Be the Day / In Spite of All the Danger*. With details of the two labels.

When Paul had the record, he digitally remastered the songs and made about 50 "facsimile" copies pressed as Christmas presents for friends. His less fortunate fans, however, had to wait until 21 November 1995, which was the release date of a first anthology, to hear the entire version of *That'll Be the Day* and another of *In Spite of All the Danger*. These were reduced to 2'45" from 3'25" of the original 78.

In any case, getting back to our story... the Quarrymen, with their first record in hand, found it was already November 1959, with no further upheavals in their virtually inexistent career. By this time, the band already had three-fourths of the lineup of the future Beatles.

George comes on the scene too

The opening night of the club owned by Mona Best turned out to be a pivotal date in the story of the future Beatles. But let us just step back in time a bit.

We mentioned changes in the lineup, and speaking of changes, in 1959 several things almost made the

**29 August 1959. Opening of the
Casbah Coffee Club.**

Quarrymen break up for good. The first was that Colin Hanton, the drummer
(a rare commodity in those days considering the cost of a drum kit), had
traumatically left the band (some say even jumping off a moving bus after a
drunken argument). The second, but also the third, and the fourth, etc., was
John Lennon's increasingly intolerant attitude towards anyone. That was it.
For one reason or another, between one argument and brawl and another, the
members of the band had dwindled down to only three, that is, John Lennon,
Paul McCartney and a certain George Harrison.

The latter had been introduced to them by a former member of the band, and
close friend of Lennon's, Pete Shotton. That was on 6 February 1958. Harrison
officially joined the band on 20 December of that year on the occasion of a
performance by the Quarrymen at the wedding of George's brother, Harry, with a
certain Irene McCann. At least that was how the story went, though there seem

29 August 1959. The first girl on the left, smiling as she watches Paul, is John's future wife Cynthia.

to be at least two other performances with George, one on 13 March, and another on 22 April 1958, at the Morgue Skiffle Cellar.

In any case, the trio Lennon-McCartney-Harrison was temporarily out of work when the bass of the Les Stewart Quartet, Ken Brown, because of an argument with the leader, Stewart himself, suddenly found he had no band for a gig they had to play. Brown was desperate and asked George if by any chance he knew of any friends who would help him out for the opening night of a new club, the Casbah. George called John and Paul, and the Quarrymen stood in for the opening night. That evening Pete, Mona Best's son, was also there. He was a drummer with a complete kit. The Beatles were again suffering from the chronic condition of being without a drummer, and Pete played with the band.

After their brilliant performance at the Casbah, the Quarrymen, joined by Ken Brown, performed again at the club on 5, 12, 19, 26 September 1959, and then on 3 and 10 October 1959. On the night of 10 October, Ken Brown had the fatal argument with "the most exclusive men's club in the world", as Paul, John and George were referred to later on. The three Quarrymen agreed unanimously to throw Ken out of the band. From that moment on, the three were no longer welcome at the Casbah either. Anything about the Beatles can always be disputed, except for the fact that the future Beatles, when it came to diplomacy, were absolutely hopeless.

That brings us to the close of 1959. It was the end of a decade and, seemingly, the end of the Quarrymen. But (in stories like this, there always seems to be a "but" at this point) a couple of things happened between October and November 1959 that seemed to put the band back on track again.

In an unspecified location, between 11 and 25 October, Johnny & the

**The first Beatles promotion card.
From left, John Lennon,
George Harrison,
Paul McCartney, and Pete Best.**

Moondogs — so now you are wondering, who are *they*? No reason to panic, they are no other than our three heroes who, for the occasion, decided to use this name — found themselves playing at the Empire Theatre again. This was for the umpteenth Carroll Levis audition for the very same TV show "Search for the Stars" from which they had been eliminated in 1957. This time the band qualified for the finals held between 26 and 31 October, again at the Empire Theatre. For the actual TV show engagement, the Quarrymen lost to a band called the Connaughts. As a consolation though, as finalists, the Quarrymen qualified to perform at the closing competitive event of the "Search for the Stars" 1959 season. This final round was held at the Manchester Hippodrome Theatre on Sunday 15 November.

A cruel and jeering twist of fate stacked the cards against them. The three Quarrymen could not afford to stay overnight in a hotel in the city, and the vote, unfortunately, was by audience "clap meter" in the presence of the artists. So, when it was the turn for Lennon, McCartney and Harrison to go onstage, they were already on the train back to Liverpool. A missed opportunity once again... what a shame.

So let us summarize the band's performances and its various lineups from 1957 until December 1959:

THE BLACK JACKS
(John Lennon, Pete Shotton)

A few duo performances in March 1957.

THE QUARRYMEN
(John Lennon, Pete Shotton, Bill Smith, Ivan Vaughan, Nigel Whalley)

Between April 1957 and early 1958
Liverpool-Garston, Wilson Hall.
Liverpool-Garston, Winter Gardens Ballroom.
Liverpool, Grafton Ballroom.
Liverpool, Locarno Ballroom.
Liverpool, Pavilion Theatre.
Liverpool, Rialto Ballroom.
Liverpool-Aintree, Pavilion Theatre.

9 June 1957
Liverpool, Empire Theatre.
Audition for the TV show "Search for the Stars".

THE QUARRYMEN
(John Lennon, Pete Shotton, Bill Smith,
Eric Griffiths, Colin Hanton, Rodney Davis,
Len Garry)

22 June 1957
Liverpool, Rosebery Street.

6 July 1957
3:00 pm
Liverpool-Woolton, St. Peter's Parish Church.
With the Band of the Cheshire
(Earl of Chester) Yeomanry.
8:00 pm
Liverpool-Woolton, St. Peter's Parish Church Hall
(without Colin Hanton).
With George Edward's Band.

July 1957 (date uncertain)
Liverpool-Woolton, Quarry Bank High School
(performance without Paul).

7 August 1957
Liverpool, Cavern Club
(performance without Paul).
With Ron McKay, the Darktown Skiffle Group,
the Deltones, the Demon Five.

18 October 1957
Liverpool-Norris Green, New Clubmoor Hall
Conservative Club (first performance with Paul).

1 November 1957
Moreton, Haig Dance Club.

7 November 1957
Liverpool-Garston, Wilson Hall.

8 November 1957
Moreton, Haig Dance Club.

15 November 1957
Moreton, Haig Dance Club.

16 November 1957
Liverpool-Old Swan,
Stanley Abattoir Social Club.

THE QUARRYMEN
(From November: John Lennon, Paul
McCartney, Len Garry, Eric Griffiths, Colin
Hanton, and occasionally John Lowe)

22 November 1957
Moreton, Haig Dance Club.

23 November 1957
Liverpool-Norris Green, New Clubmoor Hall,
Conservative Club.

28 November 1957
Moreton, Haig Dance Club.

7 December 1957
Liverpool-Garston, Wilson Hall.

Other performances during 1957
without further details:
Liverpool, St. Barnabas Church Hall.
Liverpool-Wavertree, Holyoake Hall.
Liverpool-Wavertree, Picton Road Bus
Depot Social Club.
Liverpool-Childwall, Lee Park Golf
Course Club House.
Liverpool-Childwall, Childwall Labour Club.
Liverpool-Huyton, Finch Lane Bus
Depot Social Club.
Liverpool-Gateacre, Gateacre Labour Club.

Liverpool-Ford.
Liverpool-Edge Hill, Smithdown Lane.
Bootle, St. Luke's Church Youth Club.
Prescot, Bus Depot Social Club.

10 January 1958
Liverpool-Norris Green, New Clubmoor Hall.

24 January 1958
Liverpool, Cavern Club.

6 February 1958
Liverpool-Garston, Wilson Hall.

13 March 1958
Liverpool-Broadgreen, Morgue Skiffle Cellar.
With Al Caldwell's Texans.

22 April 1958
Liverpool-Broadgreen, Morgue Skiffle Cellar.

THE QUARRYMEN
(John Lennon, Paul McCartney, George
Harrison, Colin Hanton, John Lowe)

June 1958 (date uncertain)
Liverpool-West Derby, Lowlands Club.

November-December 1958
South Manchester, Didsbury, ABC-TV Studios.

THE QUARRYMEN
(John Lennon, Paul McCartney,
George Harrison)

20 December 1958
Liverpool-Speke, 25 Upton Green.

1 January 1959
Liverpool-Garston, Wilson Hall.

24 January 1959
Liverpool-Woolton, Woolton Village Club.

THE QUARRYMEN
(John Lennon, Paul McCartney,
George Harrison, Kenneth Brown)

29 August / 5, 12, 19, 26 September /
3, 10 October 1959
Liverpool-West Derby, Casbah Coffee Club.

JOHNNY & THE MOONDOGS
(John Lennon, Paul McCartney,
George Harrison)

11 October 1959
Liverpool, Empire Theatre.
Audition for the TV show "Search for the Stars".

26, 31 October 1959
Liverpool, Empire Theatre.
Local finals for the "Search for the
Stars" TV show.

15 November 1959
Manchester-Ardwick, Hippodrome Theatre.
Evening closing event for the 1959 "Search for
the Stars" season

1960

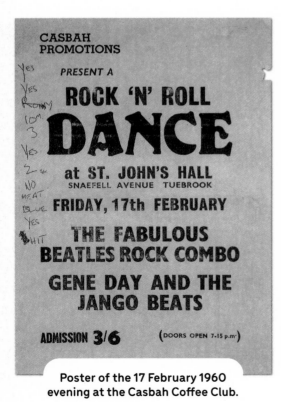

Poster of the 17 February 1960 evening at the Casbah Coffee Club.

The Silver Beatles are born

It is now January 1960. The Beatles (the band's name for now, and we will see why), from three members were now four. This was with the arrival of Stuart Sutcliffe, a friend of John Lennon's since art school. Stuart's only merit (since he was absolutely hopeless at playing a musical instrument) was to have bought a bass guitar with the money he had earned from selling one of his paintings.

The quartet performed in a series of concerts from January to May 1960 — but each time under a different name. The following is a detailed list of these performances (and names):

January
Liverpool, Liverpool College of Art School Hall. Student fete.
Performance as the Quarrymen.

10 May 1960. The Beatles audition for Larry Parnes and Billy Fury.

February
Liverpool, Cassanova Club.
Performance as the "Beatals".

23 and 24 April
Caversham, Fox & Hounds Public House.
Performance only with the duo John Lennon
and Paul McCartney as the Nerk Twins.

This abundance of different names brings us to 10 May, when after the umpteenth name change, the Quarrymen, Beatals etc. ceased to exist and became the Silver Beatles (which temporarily became the Silver *Beetles* during a tour with Johnny Gentle).

The members of the band were John Lennon, Paul McCartney, George Harrison, Stuart Sutcliffe, and the Cassanovas' drummer, Johnny Hutchinson. The latter was recruited at the last minute when their previous drummer, Thomas

Moore, left them high and dry (Moore, as in a scene from the most classic comedy, arrived in the middle of the performance...).

And so on 10 May 1960 the Silver Beatles went to audition for the band that would accompany Billy Fury on tour. Fury was a big Liverpool pop star who belonged to the stables managed by boss Larry Parnes.

When Parnes and Fury heard the Beatles, they were impressed. Yet they also both agreed that Stuart had to go. When Parnes asked if the band could play without Stuart, Lennon is said to have replied that it would be all the band or no one. And so no one it was for the Billy Fury tour, a glaring example of how to miss an opportunity by not being open to compromise. Since the band was not chosen for the Billy Fury tour, it was thought the band could play with another artist, Johnny Gentle, also a star in the Parnes stables. He would soon be going on tour to Scotland and northern England.

After the audition, the band performed another time under the unusual name of the Silver Beats:

Here and on opposite page: **Other images of the same audition. Bass guitarist Stuart Sutcliffe turned his back so that Parnes would not notice his lack of skill as a musician.**

14 May 1960
Lathom Hall, Seaforth, Liverpool.
With Cliff Roberts and the Rockers, the Deltones, King Size Taylor and the Dominoes.

After that engagement, the Beatles left on the low budget tour with Johnny Gentle that wound its way through seven dates from Friday 20 to Saturday 28 May 1960. As even the most uninformed Beatlemania fan would know, for the tour some of the Silver Beatles invented stage names for themselves. John Lennon, however, kept his own (after all, he was the leader...), but Paul McCartney became "Paul Ramon", George Harrison "Carl Harrison", Stuart Sutcliffe "Stuart de Stael". The drummer, Thomas Moore, was happy to put "Tommy" next to his real family name. Here are the details of the concerts:

20 May 1960
Afternoon
Alloa, Town Hall.
Evening
Alloa, Town Hall.
With Tommy Steele, Alex Harvey & His Beat Band, Babby Rankine.

21 May 1960
Inverness, Northern Meeting Ballroom.
With Ronnie Watt, the Chekkers Rock Dance Band.

23 May 1960
Fraserburgh, Dalrymple Hall.

25 May 1960
Keith, St. Thomas' Hall.

The contract signed on 20 May 1960 for an evening engagement of the Silver Beatles at the Grosvenor Ballroom for 6 June of that year.

26 May 1960
Forres, Town Hall.
With Rikki Barnes & His All Stars, Lena & Stevie.

27 May 1960
Nairn, Regal Ballroom.

28 May 1960
Peterhead, Rescue Hall.

The Silver Beatles spent June, July and part of August performing in a series of quite unlucrative evenings in and around Liverpool:

30 May 1960
Liverpool, Jacaranda Coffee Bar.

2 June 1960
Neston, the Institute.

4 June 1960
Liscard, Corporation's Grosvenor Ballroom.

6 June 1960
Liscard, Corporation's Grosvenor Ballroom.
With Gerry & the Pacemakers.

9 June 1960
Neston, the Institute.

11 June 1960
Liscard, Corporation's Grosvenor Ballroom
(without Thomas Moore).

13 June 1960
Liverpool, Jacaranda Coffee Bar.

10 May 1960. In the centre, Billy Fury, and on the right, Larry Parnes, as they watch the Beatles (out of range) with perplexity.

THE SILVER BEATLES
(John Lennon, Paul McCartney,
George Harrison, Stuart Sutcliffe)

16 June 1960
Neston, the Institute.
With Keith Rowlands & the Deesiders.

18 June 1960
Liscard, Corporation's Grosvenor Ballroom.

23 June 1960
Neston, the Institute.

25 June 1960
Liscard, Corporation's Grosvenor Ballroom.

30 June 1960
Neston, the Institute.

2 July 1960
Liscard, Corporation's Grosvenor Ballroom
(with Johnny Gentle).

7 July 1960
Neston, the Institute.

9 July 1960
Liscard, Corporation's Grosvenor Ballroom.

10 July 1960
Liverpool, Jacaranda Coffee Bar.
Evening as backing band for Royston Ellis.

11-15 July 1960
Liverpool, New Cabaret Artistes.
Backing band for striptease artist Janice.
Repertory performed:
The Third Man
Summertime
Moonglow and Theme from "Picnic"
September Song
It's a Long Way to Tipperary
Begin the Beguine

15 July 1960
Liverpool, New Colony Club.

THE SILVER BEATLES
(John Lennon, Paul McCartney,
George Harrison, Stuart Sutcliffe,
Norman Chapman)

16, 23 and 30 July 1960
Liscard, Corporation's Grosvenor Ballroom.

Bye bye Liverpool – Hamburg here we come!

Suddenly, the opportunity of a lifetime: "Here come The Beatles!" This was the cry of American teenagers everywhere in 1964 during the Fab Four's first tour to the U.S. In 1960, it had been announced that the name of the band would definitively be The Beatles.

During the band's final performance in Liverpool on 30 July 1960 at the Grosvenor Ballroom, the show was interrupted (or at least so the story goes) when a huge brawl broke out. There were some wounded, the police had to intervene, and as a result the venue was closed. It could only finally reopen for business under the strict condition that rock 'n' roll be prohibited from its programs. It was becoming more and more difficult, the way things were going, for the band to perform at home. And so it happened that the Beatles, persuaded by their manager Alan Williams, found themselves on 16 August 1960 on a flight

17 August 1960. The Beatles had just arrived in Hamburg and were already sent onstage at the Indra Club.

to Hamburg where they arrived at 5 pm. The members of the band were John Lennon, Paul McCartney, George Harrison, Pete Best and, finally, Stuart Sutcliffe. As you will recall, Pete Best's mother was Mona Best, the owner of the Casbah Club. And you will remember that the band took Pete Best onboard after a farce of an "audition" on 12 August. In fact, it was only because the band had been chronically out of a drummer for so long that they seized on Best.

On that 16 August 1960, they were bound for the dives of Hamburg's famous red light district, the Reeperbahn. The band was playing at the Indra Club that very evening, and would be there until 3 October. It was a gruelling feat of a total of 48 evenings and over 200 stage hours. Then, because of some of the complaints of the regulars at the Club who objected to the... noise (!) the owner – their 'employer' – Bruno Koschmider, decided to transfer the band to the Kaiserkeller, another one of Koschmider's clubs. The Beatles played at the Kaiserkeller from 4 October to 30 November 1960, for a total of 58 nights. Koschmider (whose past included the Panzerdivisionen during WWII), kept prodding them to "Mach schau!" ("Make show!"). In his mind, this meant the Beatles should be in a perpetual hysterical frenzy as they performed. The five musicians, however, after a short-lived period of reverent fear of Koschmider,

Here and on opposite page:
**17 August 1960. Onstage at the Indra Club, Paul McCartney and
John Lennon get people from the audience to participate.**

began to simply ignore their boss' ranting and raving. Indeed they remained
provocatively frozen their whole time on stage.

During that time a new club opened in Hamburg at 136 Reeperbahn. It was the
Top Ten Club, a venue of quite a different calibre than the Kaiserkeller (at least
according to Hamburg standards). The owner of the new club, Peter Eckhorn,
was determined to outdo Koschmider. He began by hiring his rival's bouncer
Horst Fascher, and then performers, singer Tony Sheridan and the Jets, who
were becoming very popular. The Beatles, who knew Sheridan, would sometimes
go to the Top Ten after their own appearances at the Kaiserkeller to watch his
shows. And not only to watch, apparently, since their boss Koschmider accused
the Beatles of breach of contract (the clause that stipulated that they could not
perform within a radius of 40 kilometres from the Kaiserkeller), Koschmider gave
the Beatles a month's notice that he was firing them for having played at the Top
Ten Club. The month's notice became much shorter than expected, thanks to
Koschmider's "tattling". He tipped off the police that the minor George Harrison,
breaking all laws in Germany, was performing in the strictly off limits quarter of
the Reeperbahn. This resulted in George being expulsed from West Germany and

sent back to Britain on 21 October. The Beatles, worried about another "close encounter" with their former "benefactor", escaped to the Top Ten Club where owner Peter Eckhorn put them up in the attic (if not out of charity, at least as a jab to his business rival).

One night, Paul and Best decided to collect their clothes and household things from the backrooms of the Bambi Kino, a third rate (third only because there was no fourth, fifth or sixth) cinema. Thanks to Koschmider's "generosity", the band had been lodged in the dressing rooms of the theatre. In their attempt to recover whatever they could in the dark, the two "burglar geniuses" thought of lighting a condom – something the Beatles were never without – and hanging it on one of the walls (according to other sources, however, the two in fact set the wallpaper on fire). Groping through the dim light, they managed to seize their things and hurry out, but completely forgot to put out the crazy lantern. The flame went out on its own in the squalid place, though this gave Koschmider the idea of accusing them of having tried to burn the cinema down. In less than an hour, McCartney was arrested by some diligent police officers and thrown in jail, and Best soon joined him. The next morning they were quite literally kicked out, and barely managed to get back to the Top Ten Club before they were arrested again and expulsed from the country.

The two musicians arrived in Liverpool on 1 December, crestfallen, exhausted and, again, out of work. The Beatles who had survived, that is, John Lennon and Stuart Sutcliffe, suddenly found themselves without their comrades-in-arms and friends. John returned to Liverpool after several adventurous exploits. Stuart's girlfriend Astrid Kirchherr let him hide out at her place, so terrorized was Stuart at the idea of being "deported".

At this point, we must make a confession. The story told up to here is in fact nothing but legend. Documents discovered in the archives of the Federal Republic of Germany and reproduced here, indicate that the Beatles in fact entered Germany with normal residence permits on all of their trips, including the first one. Yet even today, it is believed and claimed that the boys crossed the border as students on a trip. The Beatles, however, had employment contracts and work permits in hand, in addition to their residence permits. The German authorities were perfectly aware of the reason for their trip – from the day before the band's arrival in Germany – and the venue where they were performing. Above all, it was clear that Harrison was a minor and that he would be working in a club in the red-light district. As for the other myth (according to which Lennon and Sutcliffe had gone into hiding), the documents clearly show that Sutcliff had vouched for Lennon in order to keep him from being expulsed on the spot. Considering how

Paul McCartney now showing the strain of keeping up
with the infernal pace of performances.

rooted this myth is among Beatles fans, all of this documentation as a whole is of earth-shaking importance, as if, for example, an entire unreleased album by the Fab Four had suddenly been discovered! Before all of these pleasant arrests and expulsions, the Beatles had managed to do the only good thing of their entire stay in Hamburg. On 30 November they came to an agreement to perform at the Top Ten Club if their expulsion order were ever revoked.

The band's performances during this period could be summarized as follows:

THE SILVER BEATLES
(John Lennon, Paul McCartney, George Harrison, Stuart Sutcliffe, Pete Best)

12 August 1960
Liverpool, Wyvern Social Club.
Audition for a new drummer.

17 August-3 October 1960
Hamburg, Indra Club.

4 October-30 November 1960
Hamburg, Kaiserkeller.
With Rory Storm & the Hurricanes
(from 21 November without George Harrison).

End November 1960
Hamburg, Top Ten Club.
With Tony Sheridan & the Jets.

The poster announcing that the Beatles were playing from October to November 1960 in Hamburg.

The Beatles returned home again, but without Stuart. He arrived in Liverpool at the end of February 1961, only to then immediately turn around and go back to his Astrid. In the meantime, the band had begun performing at venues around Liverpool. Notably, on 27 December at the Town Hall Ballroom, where they were billed alongside the Del Renas, Searchers and Deltones.

For the first time, scenes of hysteria broke out in the audience (though the term "Beatlemania" would be coined later). And, to be quite honest, the Beatles had actually been taken for a German band. Whatever the case, this

In smart jackets on the stage of the Indra Club.
The Club, famous thanks to the Beatles, resisted the test of time
and is open still today.

resulted in McCartney and his buddies being booked for 36 concerts, from January to March 1961.

As can be seen on the amplifier behind Paul McCartney (with "The Pressmen" on it), in the early sixties the Beatles were famous for "borrowing" equipment they needed to perform onstage.

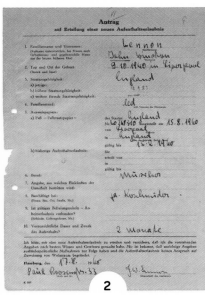

1. Kaiserkeller owner Bruno Koschmider's declaration, dated 16 August 1960, a day before the arrival of the Beatles in Hamburg. It shows that Koschmider, as well as the German police, were aware that George Harrison was a minor and that he was entering the country to work as a musician. This and the following documents disprove the belief, held true even today, that no one knew that Harrison was a minor and that the Beatles had entered Germany on tourist visas as students.
2 and 3. John Lennon's request for a residence permit dated 17 August 1960.

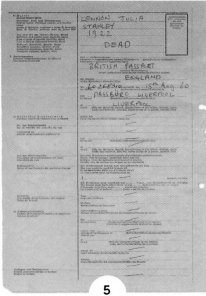

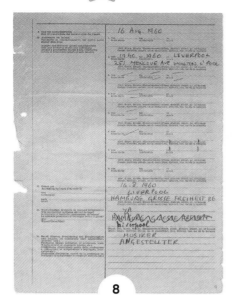

8

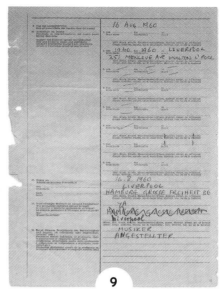

9

8 and 9. **Declarations signed by John Lennon in which he certifies that he will stay in Germany for a few days as a tourist and that he will leave the country by 10 December 1960. On Sheet 9, beneath Lennon's declaration, glued to the form (and not visible in the image) there is a declaration signed by Stuart Sutcliffe certifying that Lennon will reside at Stuart and Astrid's address during his short stay. This was all because of an expulsion order issued to the Beatles during that time.**

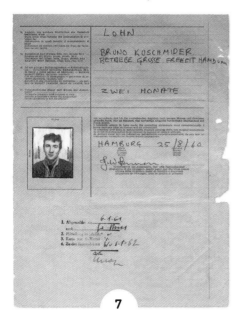

7

4, 5, 6 and 7.
The two sides of John Lennon's residence permit dated 25 August 1960. The permit indicates his profession as a musician on line 11, and the address of Koschmider's club. On the last page, an unreleased passport photo of John Lennon.

7

1961

Performances at the Cavern Club and the second Hamburg period

On 9 February 1961 the Beatles gave their debut performance at a venue by the name of... the Cavern Club. The Cavern became a second home for them and they played there hundreds of times (around 300) until August 1963. The details of their performances during the period from December 1960 until end–March 1961 are as follows:

THE BEATLES
(John Lennon, Paul McCartney, George Harrison, Pete Best, Chas Newby on bass guitar)

17 December 1960
Liverpool-West Derby, Casbah Coffee Club.

24 December 1960
Liscard, Corporation's Grosvenor Ballroom.
Christmas party.
With Derry & the Seniors.

27 December 1960
Liverpool-Litherland, Town Hall.
With the Del Renas, Searchers, Deltones.

31 December 1960
Liverpool-West Derby, Casbah Coffee Club.

THE BEATLES
(John Lennon, Paul McCartney, George Harrison, Pete Best)

5 January 1961
Liverpool-Litherland, Town Hall.

The Beatles in Hamburg during a
show at the Kaiserkeller.

1961

6 January 1961
Bootle, St. John's Hall.

7 January 1961
Liverpool-Aintree, Aintree Institute.
With Faron & the Tempest Tornadoes.

8 January 1961
Liverpool-West Derby, Casbah Coffee Club.

13 January 1961
Liverpool-Aintree, Aintree Institute.

14 January 1961
Liverpool-Aintree, Aintree Institute.
With Faron & the Tempest Tornadoes.

15 January 1961
Liverpool-West Derby, Casbah Coffee Club.

18 January 1961
Liverpool-Aintree, Aintree Institute.

19 January 1961
Liverpool-Crosby, Alexandra Hall.

20 January 1961
Liverpool-Seaforth, Lathom Hall.

21 January 1961
Liverpool-Seaforth, Lathom Hall.
Liverpool-Aintree, Aintree Institute.
With Faron & the Tempest Tornadoes.

22 January 1961
Liverpool-West Derby, Casbah Coffee Club.

25 January 1961
Liverpool Huyton, Hambleton Hall.
With Derry & the Seniors, Faron
& the Tempest Tornadoes.

26 January 1961
Liverpool-Litherland, Town Hall.

27 January 1961
Liverpool-Aintree, Aintree Institute.

28 January 1961
Liverpool-Seaforth, Lathom Hall.

Liverpool-Aintree, Aintree Institute.
With Faron & the Tempest Tornadoes.

29 January 1961
Liverpool-West Derby, Casbah Coffee Club.

30 January 1961
Liverpool-Seaforth, Lathom Hall.

1 February 1961
Liverpool-Huyton, Hambleton Hall.

2 February 1961
Liverpool-Litherland, Town Hall.

3 February 1961
Bootle, St. John's Hall.
With the Terry Owen Four.

4 February 1961
Liverpool-Seaforth, Lathom Hall.

5 February 1961
Liverpool-Walton, Blair Hall.

6 February 1961
Liverpool-Seaforth, Lathom Hall.

7 February 1961
Liverpool-Merseyside Civil Service Club.

8 February 1961
Liverpool-Aintree, Aintree Institute.

Liverpool-Huyton, Hambleton Hall.

9 February 1961
Liverpool, Cavern Club.

10 February 1961
Liverpool-Aintree, Aintree Institute.

Liverpool-Seaforth, Lathom Hall.

11 February 1961
Liverpool-Seaforth, Lathom Hall.

Liverpool, Sampson & Barlow's New Ballroom,
the Cassanova Club.

12 February 1961
Liverpool-West Derby, Casbah Coffee Club.

14 February 1961
Liverpool, Cassanova Club.
Valentine's Day Party.
With the Big Three, Rory Storm &
the Hurricanes,
Mark Peters & the Cyclones.

Liverpool-Litherland, Town Hall.
With Ray & the Del Renas with Joan.

15 February 1961
Liverpool-Aintree, Aintree Institute.
With Derry & the Seniors, Jean Day &
the Jango Beats.

Liverpool-Huyton, Hambleton Hall.
With Rory Storm & the Hurricanes,
Faron & the Tempest Tornadoes.

16 February 1961
Liverpool, Cassanova Club.

Liverpool-Litherland, Town Hall.

17 February 1961
Liverpool-Tuebrook, St. John's Hall.
With Gene Day & the Jango Beats.

18 February 1961
Liverpool-Aintree, Aintree Institute.
With the Ravens, Mark Peters & the Cyclones,
the Night Boppers.

19 February 1961
Liverpool-West Derby, Casbah Coffee Club.

21 February 1961
Liverpool, Cavern Club.

Liverpool, Cassanova Club.
With Gerry & the Pacemakers, the Big Three.

Liverpool-Litherland, Town Hall.
With Ray & the Del Renas with Joan.

22 February 1961
Liverpool-Aintree, Aintree Institute.

Liverpool-Huyton, Hambleton Hall.

24 February 1961
Liscard, Grosvenor Ballroom.

25 February 1961
Liverpool-Aintree, Aintree Institute.

Liverpool-Seaforth, Lathom Hall.
With Rory Storm & the Hurricanes,
Rikki Barnes & His All Stars.

26 February 1961
Liverpool-West Derby, Casbah Coffee Club.

28 February 1961
Liverpool, Cassanova Club.

Liverpool-Litherland, Town Hall.
With Ray & the Del Renas with Joan.

1 March 1961
Liverpool-Aintree, Aintree Institute.

2 March 1961
Liverpool-Litherland, Town Hall.
With Rory Storm & the Hurricanes, the
Dominoes.

3 March 1961
Bootle, St. John's Hall.

4 March 1961
Liverpool-Aintree, Aintree Institute.

5 March 1961
Liverpool-West Derby, Casbah Coffee Club.

6 March 1961
Liverpool, Cavern Club.

Liverpool, Liverpool Jazz Society.

7 March 1961
Liverpool, Cassanova Club.

8 March 1961
Liverpool, Cavern Club.

Liverpool-Aintree, Aintree Institute.

Liverpool-Huyton, Hambleton Hall.

10 March 1961
Liverpool, Cavern Club.

Liscard, Grosvenor Ballroom.

Liverpool-Tuebrook, St. John's Hall.

11 March 1961
Liverpool-Aintree, Aintree Institute.
With the Night Boppers, Ray & the Del Renas
with Joan, Cliff Roberts Rockers, the Ravens.

Liverpool, Liverpool Jazz Society.
With Gerry & the Pacemakers, the Remo Four,
Rory Storm & the Hurricanes, King Size Taylor &
the Dominoes, the Big Three, Dale Roberts & the
Jaywalkers, Derry & the Seniors, Ray & the Del
Renas, the Pressmen, Johnny Rocco & the Jets,
Faron & the Tempest Tornadoes.

12 March 1961
Liverpool, Cassanova Club.
With King Size Taylor & the Dominoes.

13 March 1961
Liverpool, Liverpool Jazz Society.

14 March 1961
Liverpool, Cavern Club.

15 March 1961
Liverpool, Cavern Club.

Liverpool, Liverpool Jazz Society.
With Gerry & the Pacemakers, Rory Storm & the
Wild Ones.

16 March 1961
Liverpool, Cavern Club.

17 March 1961
Liverpool-Croxteth, Mossway Hall.

Liverpool, Liverpool Jazz Society.

19 March 1961
Liverpool-West Derby, Casbah Coffee Club.

20 March 1961
Liverpool, Cavern Club.

Liverpool-Huyton, Hambleton Hall.
With the Ravens.

21 March 1961
Liverpool, Cavern Club.
With the Bluegenes, the Remo Four, Dale
Roberts & the Jaywalkers.

22 March 1961
Liverpool, Cavern Club.

24 March 1961
Liverpool, Cavern Club.

26 March 1961
Liverpool-West Derby, Casbah Coffee Club.

The Beatles finally started to become popular at home. After that last concert, thanks to the help of Best's mother Mona, and Eckhorn, the Beatles obtained an annulment of their orders of expulsion. This good news came at a time when, with the inexorable passing of time, George Harrison had finally turned 18 on 25 February 1961. The band's return to Hamburg was feasible, and indeed, they returned to perform at the Top Ten Club from 1 April to 1 July 1961, for a total of 13 weeks, that is, 98 nights, or 53 hours on stage.

Some other important events also occurred during this busy period. Firstly, Stuart – as he wrote in a letter to his mother on 31 April 1961, after the band's second trip to Hamburg – decided to definitively leave the Beatles. He wanted to devote himself to his great passion which was painting and decided to enrol in the Academy of Fine Arts (tragically, however, Stuart died at only 21 years of age, on 10 April 1962 in Hamburg, of a cerebral haemorrhage).

While Stuart was still with the band, he was destined to make a landmark contribution to the history of the Fab Four. Indeed, it was during that period that Astrid changed her boyfriend's haircut and gave him the drastic moptop that would become universally known as the "Beatles cut". When the other four members of the band first caught sight of Stuart, though, they found him absolutely hilarious. Yet, a little while later, on second thought, they too soon rushed to do the same – all except Pete Best, who kept his Elvis tuft.

The important second event during this time was the band's recording of a disc on 22 and 24 June. This was as backing band for Tony Sheridan (yes, precisely the same artist they had worked with on their first trip to Hamburg). With Sheridan and the label Polydor, the band recorded *My Bonnie*, *When the Saints…*, *Why*,

Nobody's Child, If You Love Me Baby (for which the Beatles, without Stuart, did backing vocals for Sheridan), and *Ain't She Sweet* (sung by John).

The band's first single release was an instrumental by a rare Lennon-Harrison duo entitled *Cry for a Shadow* and on the B side, *When the Saints* (though the label read "Tony Sheridan and the Beat Brothers"). The record climbed to fifth on the charts and sold about 100,000 copies. Its success was due above all to the Beatles, who had by now become quite famous. An interesting aside about the disc was that Polydor apparently refused to use the name 'Beatles' for it, since it sounded too much like 'Peetles', slang for penis...

Another notable occurrence during this period was that Paul's Rosetti guitar finally gave up the ghost. McCartney had to perform on the piano instead, or simply as vocalist, since apparently he refused to play Stuart's Hofner Bass — or at least if he did, only sporadically, and there are no photos proving this.

The financial "tragedy" this loss represented, however, forced Paul to buy the bass guitar that over the years would become his legendary trademark: the Hofner Violin Bass. Paul bought the instrument at the local Hamburg Steinway Music Shop, though reluctantly, being he was as tight-fisted as ever.

**April 1961. The Beatles at the Top Ten
Club with Tony Sheridan.**

The Beatles returned to Liverpool on 4 July 1961, which was a Monday, ready to definitively make history. Here exhibited is something extraordinary for your admiration. It is a receipt written on a sheet torn from an accounts book of the Top Ten Club, dated 17 to 23 June 1961, and with the heading "Musiken-Gehalter" ("Musicians' Fees"). The receipt, handwritten in blue, and in German, lists the five Beatles plus Tony Sheridan (whose signature is missing) in the following order: George Harrison, Paul McCartney, John Lennon, Stuart Sutcliffe, Pete Best and Tony Sheridan. The details of their fees were: "7 Tage x 35 = DM 245" (7 days at 35 DM) which, less taxes, gives a total net per week of 215 DM for each Beatle.

This find is very important in the history of the Beatles, since it refers to the

A Beatles "payslip" for performances in Hamburg.

very week that the Beatles made the previously mentioned recordings with Tony Sheridan.

Here are the details of the band's second stay in Hamburg:

27 March-2 July 1961
Hamburg, Top Ten Club.
Occasionally as backing band for Tony Sheridan,
and appearances with Stuart Sutcliffe on bass.

Meeting 'Mr. Epstein'

When the Beatles returned to Liverpool after their second trip to Hamburg, they had something valuable in hand. At the time, they did not realise it, but this would have tremendous impact on the band's future.

We are of course referring to that single recorded in Hamburg. At the time — in July 1961 — nothing could have foretold the extraordinary upheaval this record would cause. Yet, in just about three months...

Brian Epstein contributed tremendously to the success of the Beatles and in return received unprecedented fame as a music entrepeneur and manager.

So, as we were saying, the Beatles had come back from Hamburg, richer for the glory of it, but above all, for the experience gained. All of those hours spent onstage in that pleasant German city had served as excellent training and had made them into incredibly polished performers.

John Lennon in Hamburg.

George Harrison in Hamburg. In the background, the blurred faces of John Lennon and Paul McCartney. By this time, all of the Beatles except Pete Best had adopted the "Beatles cut".

They were basking in glory yes, but not without limits. In fact they were only really famous within the perimeters of Liverpool and its outskirts. And some in Liverpool had even once confused them with a German band! But destiny by now had put the gears in motion, and the momentum would never stop...

In July something occurred that would greatly affect the course of the Beatles' career: a certain Bill Harry created a magazine-type newspaper dedicated to music called *Mersey Beat*. The publication devoted a lot of space to news on local bands and, of course, to the biggest stars of the city (musically speaking), and so, precisely, the Beatles.

So here was a newspaper interested in the Beatles and the single they had just wrapped up. In the second issue, a bold headline appeared on the first page: "Beatles sign recording contract!" Great publicity, it goes without saying, but it would have ended there, if the article had not been noticed by a certain Mr. Brian Epstein, creator of the record department of NEMS (North End Music Store).

Here we must pause and indulge in a fascinating digression. Yes, because here was a certain twenty-seven-year-old, who after quite a turbulent youth, was about to burst into the world of the Beatles like a tornado.

Brian Epstein was born in Liverpool on 19 September 1934. He was the son of Harry Epstein and Malka Hyman, who belonged to the wealthy Jewish bourgeoisie of the city. Brian enjoyed a happy carefree existence until September 1950, when at sixteen, according to family tradition, being the eldest son he was sent to work in his father's store. There, he showed himself to be among the business' best sales people... that is, of kitchen tables.

In 1952, Brian was drafted into Her Majesty's Army. After a period of training he was sent to London and the barracks at Regent's Park. Being that this was

Under the guidance of Brian Epstein, the Beatles began to change their dress code from black leather to jackets and ties.

a depot for equipment for the British infantry, it was an easy assignment. Yet after a year, when he still had another year to complete his service, the young Brian was suddenly dismissed for rather vague reasons. The Army nevertheless recognised him as 'serious, conscientious, and always deserving of the utmost confidence'. With this curious discharge, Brian returned to Liverpool and was sent to work in the record department of the NEMS music store owned by the Epstein family. It seemed the perfect job had been found for Brian. With his great passion for classical music, he succeeded in making the store flourish. That is, until his poor parents were faced with another calamity. Indeed, Brian suddenly announced to them in great pomp that he had decided to enrol in classes at the RADA, the London Royal Academy of Dramatic Art. Yet after about a year, Brian gave up this idea too, living up to his reputation as a true "weathervane", as his grandfather Isaac always described him. He returned to Liverpool much to the great relief of his parents, and was immediately assigned to a family store, in the position of manager.

By 1957 Brian was well into living a double life. He was the young successful businessman by day, but after dark, was a regular of "the Storch", a longstanding haunt of the young gay crowd of Liverpool.

From 1958 to 1961, despite a few mishaps that even took Brian to court – to testify in a trial concerning the homosexual underworld of Liverpool – he succeeded in making the entire music branch of his father's company into a thriving business. NEMS now boasted two highly popular stores known for records, instruments and music equipment. "Mr. Epstein of NEMS", was how Brian was known in Liverpool's music circles. It was therefore only normal that the editor-in-chief of *Mersey Beat*, Bill Harry, would approach him to be a regular contributor to his publication. The newspaper was sold in all the NEMS outlets of the city.

And this is where the paths of the Beatles and Mr. Epstein crossed. Legend has it that at 3:00 pm on 28 October 1961, the young man, Raymond Jones, went to the NEMS store at White Chapel. Mr. Epstein happened to be behind the counter and Raymond asked for the record by the Beatles – specifying "Beatles with an 'a'" – entitled *My Bonnie*. This request was what sparked Brian's curiosity in the band.

This is how the story goes, but it was probably more likely that Brian already knew about the Beatles. After all, they had had regular coverage in the pop music newspaper *Mersey Beat* that was sold in his stores. The Beatles had even been featured on the cover of the second issue. Perhaps it was precisely the whimsical qualities of a "weathervane", as Brian's grandfather Isaac liked to describe his grandson, that could explain Brian's interest in these four musicians who were such a far cry from his world.

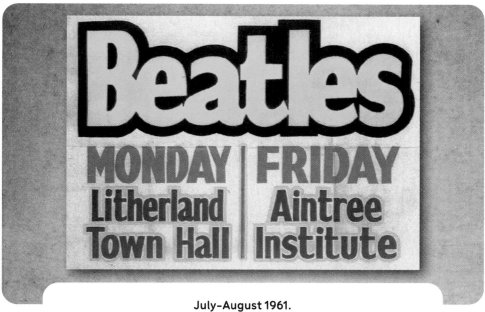

July–August 1961.
Poster for two Beatles concerts.

The Beatles continued to play at the Cavern, but also in any venues that would have them. This was the period from 13 July, the day of their first performance after returning home from Hamburg on 3 July, to 9 November, a date that marked a true turning point in their career. Here is a summary of the performances during that period:

13 July 1961
Liverpool-Tuebrook, St. John's Hall.

14 July 1961
Afternoon
Liverpool, Cavern Club.
Evening
Liverpool, Cavern Club.
With Johnny Sandon & the Searchers.

15 July 1961
Liverpool-Wavertree, Holyoake Hall.

16 July 1961
Liverpool-Walton, Blair Hall.

17 July 1961
Afternoon
Liverpool, Cavern Club.
Evening
Liverpool-Litherland, Town Hall.
With Gerry & the Pacemakers.

19 July 1961
Liverpool, Cavern Club.

The Beatles again at the Cavern Club.
Behind them the famous wall of the Club
where singers etched their names.
Years later, John Lennon would refer
to these as "artistic graffiti".

20 July 1961
Liverpool-Tuebrook, St. John's Hall.

21 July 1961
Afternoon
Liverpool, Cavern Club.
Evening
Liverpool-Aintree, Aintree Institute.
With Cy & the Cimarrons.

22 July 1961
Liverpool-Wavertree, Holyoake Hall.

23 July 1961
Liverpool-Walton, Blair Hall.

24 July 1961
Liverpool-Litherland, Town Hall.

25 July 1961
Afternoon
Liverpool, Cavern Club.
Evening
Liverpool, Cavern Club.
With the Bluegenes, Gerry & the Pacemakers,
the Remo Four, the Four Jays.

26 July 1961
Liverpool, Cavern Club.
With the Remo Four, the Four Jays.

27 July 1961
Afternoon
Liverpool, Cavern Club.
Evening
Liverpool-Tuebrook, St. John's Hall.
With Cilla White, the Big Three, the Strangers.

28 July 1961
Liverpool-Aintree, Aintree Institute.
With the Strangers.

29 and 30 July 1961
Liverpool-Walton, Blair Hall.

31 July 1961
Afternoon
Liverpool, Cavern Club.
Evening
Liverpool-Litherland, Town Hall.

2 August 1961
Liverpool, Cavern Club.

3 August 1961
Liverpool-Tuebrook, St. John's Hall.

4 August 1961
Afternoon
Liverpool, Cavern Club.
Evening
Liverpool-Aintree, Aintree Institute.
With Cy & the Cimarrons.

5 August 1961
Liverpool, Cavern Club.
With the Remo Four, Kenny Ball's Jazzmen,
Mike Cotton's Jazzmen.

6 August 1961
Liverpool-West Derby, Casbah Coffee Club.

7 August 1961
Liverpool-Litherland, Town Hall.

8 and 9 August 1961
Liverpool, Cavern Club.

10 August 1961
Afternoon
Liverpool, Cavern Club.
Evening
Liverpool-Tuebrook, St. John's Hall.

1961

11 August 1961
Liverpool, Cavern Club.

12 August 1961
Liverpool-Aintree, Aintree Institute.

13 August 1961
Liverpool-West Derby, Casbah Coffee Club.

14 and 16 August 1961
Liverpool, Cavern Club.

17 August 1961
Liverpool-Tuebrook, St. John's Hall,
With Johnny Gustafson, the Big Three,
the Comets.

18 August 1961
Afternoon
Liverpool, Cavern Club.
Evening
Liverpool-Aintree, Aintree Institute.
With Steve Bennett & the Syndicate.

19 August 1961
Liverpool-Aintree, Aintree Institute.

20 August 1961
Liverpool-Huyton, Hambleton Hall.

21 and 23 August 1961
Liverpool, Cavern Club.

24 August 1961
Liverpool-Tuebrook, St. John's Hall.

25 August 1961
Afternoon
Liverpool, Cavern Club.
Evening
Mersey River, show onboard the boat
the "Royal Iris". With Mr. Acker Bilk's
Paramount Jazz Band.

26 August 1961
Liverpool-Aintree, Aintree Institute.

27 August 1961
West Derby, Casbah Coffee Club.

28, 29 and 30 August 1961
Liverpool, Cavern Club.

31 August 1961
Liverpool-Tuebrook, St. John's Hall.

1 September 1961
Afternoon
Liverpool, Cavern Club.
With Karl Terry & the Cruisers.
Evening
Liverpool, Cavern Club.
With Dizzy Burton's Jazz Band.

2 September 1961
Liverpool-Aintree, Aintree Institute.

3 September 1961
Liverpool-Huyton, Hambleton Hall.

5 September 1961
Liverpool, Cavern Club.
With the Bluegenes, the Remo Four,
Gerry & the Pacemakers.

6 September 1961
Liverpool, Cavern Club.
With Ian & the Zodiacs, Johnny Sandon
& the Searchers.

7 September 1961
Afternoon
Liverpool, Cavern Club.
Evening
Liverpool-Litherland, Town Hall.

8 September 1961
Liverpool-Tuebrook, St. John's Hall.

9 September 1961
Liverpool-Aintree, Aintree Institute.

10 September 1961
Liverpool-West Derby, Casbah Coffee Club.

11 September 1961
Liverpool, Cavern Club.

Here and on opposite page:
**The afternoon of
8 December 1961.
The Beatles perform at the
Cavern Club as backing band
for singer Davy Jones.**

13 September 1961
Afternoon
Liverpool, Cavern Club.
Evening
Liverpool, Cavern Club.
With the Remo Four, the Pressmen.

14 September 1961
Liverpool-Litherland, Town Hall.

15 September 1961
Afternoon
Liverpool, Cavern Club.
Evening
Liscard, Grosvenor Ballroom.
With Cliff Roberts & the Rockers.

Liverpool-Knotty Ash, Village Hall.

16 September 1961
Liverpool-Aintree, Aintree Institute.

17 September 1961
Liverpool-Huyton, Hambleton Hall.

19 September 1961
Liverpool, Cavern Club.

20 September 1961
Liverpool, Cavern Club.
With Ian & the Zodiacs, Karl Terry & the
Cruisers.

21 September 1961
Afternoon
Liverpool, Cavern Club.
Evening
Liverpool-Litherland, Town Hall.
Con Gerry & the Pacemakers, Rory Storm
& the Hurricanes.

22 September 1961
Liverpool-Knotty Ash, Village Hall.

23 September 1961
Liverpool-Aintree, Aintree Institute.

24 September 1961
Liverpool-West Derby, Casbah Coffee Club.

25 and 27 September 1961
Liverpool, Cavern Club.

28 September 1961
Liverpool-Litherland, Town Hall.

29 September 1961
Afternoon
Liverpool, Cavern Club.
Evening
Liverpool-Knotty Ash, Village Hall.

15 October 1961
Afternoon
Liverpool-Maghull, Albany Cinema.
With Hank Walters & the Dusty Road Ramblers,
Les Arnold, Joe Cordova, Dave Dunn & Jim
Markey, Lennie Rens, Shirley Gordon, Bert King,
the Eltones, Ken Dodd, Denis Smerdon, Edna
Bell, Jackie Owen & the Joe Royal Trio.
Evening
Liverpool-Huyton, Hambleton Hall.

16 October 1961
Liverpool, Cavern Club.

17 October 1961
Liverpool, David Lewis Club.
First concert for the "Beatles Fan Club".

18 October 1961
Afternoon
Liverpool, Cavern Club.
Evening
Liverpool, Cavern Club.
With the Four Jays, Ian & the Zodiacs.

19 October 1961
Liverpool-Litherland, Town Hall.
With Gerry & the Pacemakers,
Karl Terry & the Cruisers.
The Beatles performed with Gerry & the
Pacemakers & Karl Terry under the name
"the Beatmakers".

20 October 1961
Afternoon
Liverpool, Cavern Club.
Evening
Liverpool-Knotty Ash, Village Hall.

Here and on opposite page:
**Other photos at the Cavern.
In this series, we note Paul
McCartney who plays seated
during the singer's famous
Little Richard imitation.**

Davy Jones again on 8 December 1961. But this time in the evening.
The quilted backdrop tells us the photo was taken at the
Tower Ballroom.

21 October 1961
Two concerts.
Liverpool, Cavern Club.

22 October 1961
Liverpool-West Derby, Casbah Coffee Club.

24, 25 and 26 October 1961
Liverpool, Cavern Club.

27 October 1961
Liverpool-Knotty Ash, Village Hall.

28 October 1961
Liverpool-Aintree, Aintree Institute.

29 October 1961
Liverpool-Huyton, Hambleton Hall.

30 October 1961
Liverpool, Cavern Club.

31 October 1961
Liverpool-Litherland, Town Hall.

1, 3 and 4 November 1961
Liverpool, Cavern Club.

5 November 1961
Southport, Glenpark Club.

6 November 1961
Manchester, Three Coins Club.

7 November 1961
Afternoon
Liverpool, Cavern Club.
Evening
Liverpool, Merseyside Civil Service
Club and Liverpool, Cavern Club.

8 November 1961
Liverpool, Cavern Club.

9 November 1961
Afternoon
Liverpool, Cavern Club.
(Brian Epstein comes to see the show).
Evening
Liverpool-Litherland, Town Hall.

And so, on that 'glorious' (at least in the history of music) 9 November, Mr. Epstein arranged to go to the Cavern for the first time. He saw to all the details of his visit to make sure it would all go smoothly. First Brian gave a call to Bill Harry, the editor of *Mersey Beat*, and asked that Ray McFall, the owner of the Cavern, be advised that he was coming. McFall, as in the most classic chain of command, ordered his bouncer, Paddy Delaney, to keep an eye out for Brian and when he arrived, to show him straight into the Club.

And so on 9 November, just a little before the noon show, Brian Epstein made his quite unimpressive entrance into the Cavern. The place was as smokey, gritty and smelly as ever. His presence was announced over the microphone by the Club's DJ, Bob Wooler. And that was it.

This was how Brian saw the Beatles perform for the first time. During the break Brian went to introduce himself to the band. He received a "warm" welcome in the form of a question from George whose tone was somewhere between ironic and sneery, "What brings Mr. Epstein here?" A million pound question, indeed, since at that point not even Brian himself had any idea why he was there.

In any case, after a short chat with Paul, he found out that *My Bonnie/The Saints* had been released by Polydor. With this information he could order two hundred copies for the NEMS store. Brian continued going to the Cavern and was accompanied by Alistair Taylor, his personal assistant.

Later Alistair became part of the Beatles' large support group and crew consisting of a road manager, assistants, and general staff. During the weeks that followed, there were various other encounters and meetings, and these culminated on 24 January 1962 in the signature of a contract between Epstein

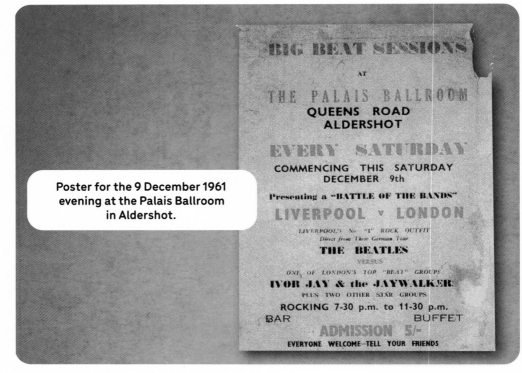

BIG BEAT SESSIONS

AT

THE PALAIS BALLROOM

QUEENS ROAD
ALDERSHOT

EVERY SATURDAY

COMMENCING THIS SATURDAY
DECEMBER 9th

Presenting a "BATTLE OF THE BANDS"

LIVERPOOL v LONDON

LIVERPOOL'S No. "1" ROCK OUTFIT
Direct from Their German Tour

THE BEATLES

VERSUS

ONE OF LONDON'S TOP "BEAT" GROUPS

IVOR JAY & the JAYWALKERS

PLUS TWO OTHER STAR GROUPS

ROCKING 7-30 p.m. to 11-30 p.m.

BAR   BUFFET

ADMISSION 5/-

EVERYONE WELCOME—TELL YOUR FRIENDS

Poster for the 9 December 1961
evening at the Palais Ballroom
in Aldershot.

and the Beatles in the NEMS offices. A contract that Brian... forgot to sign.

Actually he only put this right three days before the Beatles' recording debut on 2 October 1962. It was at this time that two witnesses and the guardians of two of the Beatles who were still minors were present. (At the time, the age of majority in the U.K. was 21). These were Paul's and George's respective fathers. It was only then that the contract became effective.

The contract between the Beatles and Brian was binding for five years, in exchange for a percentage due to the manager of 25%.

During that December other events also occurred that were destined to affect the course of the Beatles' career. Brian, as the band's zealous 'future manager', decided to contact music critic Tony Barrow. Barrow, under the pen name Disker, had a regular review column in the *Liverpool Echo*. Though he wrote for the publication in Liverpool, he lived in London. Brian left for the capital to meet him after receiving a response from Barrow, and had the critic listen to a demo. This resulted in getting the contact of "somebody" at Decca Records (the record company for which Barrow worked alongside his activity as journalist).

To be quite honest, however, Decca's sole concern was above all not to do anything to antagonize the owner of NEMS. The store was one of Decca's largest record outlets in Northern England. This explains how it happened that Dick Rowe, the head of A&R at Decca, decided to ask his assistant, Mike Smith, to go to Liverpool on 13 December to watch a performance of the Beatles at the Cavern Club.

Smith, obeying instructions, arrived in Liverpool and was welcomed by Epstein in great style. After "bribing" him with a lavish lunch, he took Smith to the Cavern to see the show. Smith greatly liked the performance, even to the point of organizing an audition of the Beatles at the Decca studios on Monday 1 January 1962.

Things were finally moving!

Details of the Beatles' performances during the period from 10 November 1961 (date of Epstein's first visit to the Cavern) to 1 January 1962 (day of "the Decca audition" as it came to be known) are as follows:

10 November 1961
7:30 pm-1:00 am
New Brighton, Tower Ballroom.
"Operation Big Beat 1"
With Gerry & the Pacemakers, Rory Storm & the Hurricanes,
the Remo Four, King Size Taylor & the Dominoes.
10:30 pm-11:00 pm
Liverpool-Knotty Ash, Village Hall.

N.B. "Operation Big Beat 1" was a big show organised in Liverpool by Sam Leach (an impresario known for his interest in promoting this type of production and who actively pursued this activity for many years). The show featured what were considered Liverpool's most popular bands.

Lewisohn's *Chronicle* points out that an advertisement promoting the evening event appeared in the *Liverpool Echo* on 27 October. It indicated the NEMS as the authorized pre-sales point. This fact prompted Lewisohn to perhaps rather hastily assume that Epstein knew of the band at least 24 hours before 28 October. That was the day, it is related, that Raymond Jones went to the NEMS store and asked Brian for the Beatles single.

Yet, on the other hand, Brian's store was one of the biggest in Liverpool. It was the authorized pre-sales point for almost all of the music events organised in the city. Epstein would not necessarily have noticed the Beatles' name, particularly since they were billed with many bands more famous than they.

11 November 1961
Liverpool-Aintree, Aintree Institute.

12 November 1961
Liverpool-Huyton, Hambleton Hall.
Beatles Beat Show.
With the Rockin' Climbers, Jimmy & the
Midnighters, Faron & the Flamingos.

13 November 1961
Liverpool, Cavern Club.

14 November 1961
Liverpool, Merseyside Civil Service Club.

Liverpool, Cavern Club.

15 November 1961
Liverpool, Starline Club.

17 November 1961
Afternoon
Liverpool, Cavern Club.
Evening
Liverpool-Knotty Ash, Village Hall.

18 November 1961
Liverpool, Cavern Club.

19 November 1961
Liverpool-West Derby, Casbah Coffee Club.

21 November 1961
Afternoon
Liverpool, Cavern Club.
Evening
Liverpool, Merseyside Civil Service Club.

22 and 23 November 1961
Liverpool, Cavern Club.

24 November 1961
Liverpool-West Derby, Casbah Coffee Club.

7:30 pm – 2:00 am
New Brighton, Tower Ballroom.
Operation Big Beat 2
(two songs with Davy Jones).
With Emile Ford, Davy Jones, Rory Storm & the
Hurricanes, Gerry & the Pacemakers, the Remo
Four, Earl Preston & the Tempest Tornadoes,
Faron & the Flamingos.

26 November 1961
Liverpool-Huyton, Hambleton Hall.

27 November 1961
Liverpool, Cavern Club.

28 November 1961
Liverpool, Merseyside Civil Service Club.

29 November 1961
Liverpool, Cavern Club.

1 December 1961
Afternoon
Liverpool, Cavern Club.
Evening
New Brighton, Tower Ballroom.
With Rory Storm & the Hurricanes,
Dale Roberts & the Jaywalkers, King Size Taylor
& the Dominoes, Derry & the Seniors,
Steve Day & the Drifters.

2 December 1961
Liverpool, Cavern Club.

3 December 1961
Liverpool-West Derby, Casbah Coffee Club.

5 and 6 December 1961
Liverpool, Cavern Club.

**The Beatles during a break
at the Cavern Club.**

8 December 1961
Afternoon
Liverpool, Cavern Club
(as backing band for Davy Jones).
Evening
New Brighton, Tower Ballroom,
Davy Jones Show (as backing band for Davy
Jones). With Danny Williams, Davy Jones, Rory
Storm & the Hurricanes, Gerry & the Pacemakers,
the Remo Four, Earl Preston & the TT's.

9 December 1961
7:30 pm -11:30 pm
Aldershot, the Palais Ballroom.
"Battle of the Bands".
With Ivor Jay & the Jaywalkers.
1:00 pm
London-Soho, the Blue Gardenia Club
(without George Harrison).

10 December 1961
Liverpool-Huyton, Hambleton Hall.

11 and 13 December 1961
Liverpool, Cavern Club.

15 December 1961
Afternoon
Liverpool, Cavern Club.
Evening
New Brighton, Tower Ballroom.
With Cass & the Cassanovas, Rory Storm &
the Hurricanes, Derry & the Seniors,
Dale Roberts & the Jaywalkers, the Big Three.

16 December 1961
Liverpool, Cavern Club.
With the Saints Jazz Band, Micky Ashman's
Ragtime Jazz Band, the White Eagles Jazz Band.

**Photos of the disastrous performance of
9 December 1961 at the Palais Ballroom in Aldershot.
There was a total of 18 non-paying spectators present.
The half empty dance floor in the above photo
speaks for itself...**

17 December 1961
Liverpool-West Derby, Casbah Coffee Club.

18 and 19 December 1961
Liverpool, Cavern Club.

20 December 1961
Liverpool, Cavern Club.
With the Strangers, Mark Peters & the Cyclones.

21 December 1961
Liverpool, Cavern Club.

23 December 1961
Liverpool, Cavern Club.
With the Saints Jazz Band, Micky Ashman's
Ragtime Jazz Band.

24 December 1961
Liverpool-West Allerton, Allerton Synagogue.

26 December 1961
New Brighton, Tower Ballroom.

27 December 1961
Liverpool, Cavern Club.
The Beatles Christmas Party.
With Gerry & the Pacemakers,
King Size Taylor & the Dominoes.

29 December 1961
Liverpool, Cavern Club.
With the Yorkshire Jazz Band.

30 December 1961
Liverpool, Cavern Club.
With Gerry & the Pacemakers.

At 12:00 noon on 31 December 1961, in an icy England, a van trudged on with its charge of four musicians, their instruments, and a driver who was not too sure where he was going. After ten hours on the road, most of the time struggling against a snowstorm, the Beatles and their driver and jack-of-all-trades, Neil Aspinall, arrived in London at the frenetic height of New Year's preparations. Brian Epstein had gone on ahead by train the day before, and was staying with an aunt.

The morning of January 1st, the Beatles arrived at the Decca studios. However, Mike Smith, still recovering from the festivities, was nowhere in sight. Epstein exploded for the umpteenth time taking this as a personal snub from Smith. Finally at around 11:00 am, the Beatles could begin the audition.

They recorded fifteen songs on a two-track tape: *Like Dreamers Do; Money (That's What I Want); Till There Was You; The Sheik of Araby; To Know Her Is to Love Her; Take Good Care of My Baby; Memphis Tennessee; Sure to Fall (In Love with You); Hello Little Girl; Three Cool Cats; Crying, Waiting, Hoping; Love of the Loved; September in the Rain; Besame Mucho;* and *Searchin'.*

For starters, Smith had decreed straightaway that their "things" (referring to the amplifiers) would in no way do. He gave the order to connect their instruments up to the studio amps.

At the end of the recording session, Smith nevertheless personally told Brian and the Beatles that it had all gone well. The band and Brian went out to celebrate with dinner in a restaurant in the upmarket Swiss Cottage neighbourhood. At that very moment, however, at Decca it was decided that since on that same day another band, Brian Poole and the Tremeloes, had recorded a good demo, and since this band was based in the outskirts of London, there was no point in signing a band from Liverpool. Moreover (in Decca's opinion) the Liverpool band seemed too similar to the Shadows.

After an affirmation that will go down in history as the biggest miscalculation second only to considering the Titanic unsinkable, the two Decca employees Dick Rowe and Beecher Stevens informed a speechless Brian that "groups with guitars are on their way out, Mr. Epstein..."

Not even Brian's offer to buy 3,000 copies of every record the Beatles made could get the Company's managers to change their minds. And thus Decca's decision earned them first place on the charts of the most foolish company of all time in the history of the music industry.

Here and on opposite page: **9 December 1961. The Beatles before, during, and after their performance at the Palais Ballroom in Aldershot. John Lennon smirks and makes grotesque faces to relieve the tension of the evening's flop.**

1962

Looking for a recording contract

On 5 January 1962 Polydor released the single *My Bonnie / The Saints* (Polydor NH 66833), which became the first English single under the name of The Beatles. Of course, sales were very sparse and all limited to the Liverpool area. In the meantime, although Brian had still not digested Decca's rejection, he began a series of London "pilgrimages" in the attempt to propose the band to other record companies. The only result was a curt "no" from Pye, and Oriole as well. Brian's friend Bob Boast (whom he had met in Hamburg during a sales management seminar) was head of the HMV stores. Yet on 8 February 1962, even Boast told Brian that unfortunately he could do nothing for them. Seeing the

The record *My Bonnie*, Tony Sheridan & Beatles.

29 March 1962.
The Beatles at the Old Spot Club.
The band performs in suits and
ties bought by Brian Epstein to
replace their – according to him –
inappropriate leather outfits.

At the Star–Club in Hamburg.

afflicted expression on Epstein's face, Boast suggested that he go to the floor above the HMV store on Oxford Street. There was an acetate recording service there open to the public and Brian would be able to transfer the tapes of the Decca session to disc.

There are times when situations in real life surpass by far anything we could ever imagine. How else can we explain the fact that an employee, such as Jim Foy, happened to be working precisely at the recording service where he was responsible for transferring customers' tapes to disc. And that the tape Jim was transferring for Brian suddenly aroused his interest to the point that he suggested to the nice worried gentleman to try contacting Sid Coleman, manager of Ardmore and Beechwood, an EMI music publishing subsidiary...

It was evident to Sid Coleman that the Beatles and Epstein himself were adrift, that they had no recording contract in hand and were looking for concrete solutions for their future. He contacted the people at Parlophone (another EMI label) and asked to speak with "the boss", George Martin.

Martin was not there and an appointment was set up at the EMI headquarters on Manchester Square for Tuesday 13 February. The next day, on 9 February,

Coleman and Epstein came to an agreement in principle concerning the rights of the music publications and finally, on 13 February, Martin and Epstein met at EMI. The Beatles' music stirred somewhat of an interest in George Martin who raised his right eyebrow for a fleeting moment... George Martin thought the Beatles deserved more consideration and also that they be heard live, but that was it. He threw the usual "We'll call *you*" at Epstein, and left the budding manager in torment, torn between hope and bitterness.

Still stinging from the disappointment of the Decca rejection, the Beatles and Brian threw themselves headlong into their work. Epstein actually managed to get some good engagements for the band during that time.

These brought them up a notch from their usual routine at the Cavern Club (where they nevertheless continued to perform regularly), or some of the seedy clubs where they played (and where there was always the risk the night might end up in a merry brawl among some of the rough customers there). This was all the norm for the band, that is, until April 1962. Here are details of their performances during that period:

**Still very young,
but starting to flex their muscles...**

3 and 5 January 1962
Liverpool, Cavern Club.

6 January 1962
Liverpool, Cavern Club.
With the Collegians.

7 January 1962
Liverpool-West Derby, Casbah Coffee Club.

9 January 1962
Liverpool, Cavern Club.

10 January 1962
Liverpool, Cavern Club.
With Gerry & the Pacemakers, the Strangers.

11 January 1962
Liverpool, Cavern Club.

12 January 1962
Liverpool, Cavern Club.
With Mike Cotton's Jazzmen.

New Brighton, Tower Ballroom,
With Mel Turner & the Bandits, Rory Storm
& the Hurricanes, the Strangers,
Mr. Twist & the Twistettes.

13 January 1962
Liverpool-Huyton, Hambleton Hall.

14 January 1962
Liverpool-West Derby, Casbah Coffee Club.

15 January 1962
Liverpool, Cavern Club.

17 January 1962
Afternoon
Liverpool, Cavern Club.
Evening
Liverpool, Cavern Club.
With the Remo Four, Ian & the Zodiacs.

19 January 1962
Afternoon
Liverpool, Cavern Club.
Evening
New Brighton, Tower Ballroom.

20 January 1962
Liverpool, Cavern Club.

21 January 1962
Liverpool-West Derby, Casbah Coffee Club.

22 January 1962
Afternoon
Liverpool, Cavern Club.
Evening
Southport, Kingsway Club.

24 January 1962
Liverpool, Cavern Club.

26 January 1962
Afternoon
Liverpool, Cavern Club.
Evening
Liverpool, Cavern Club.
New Brighton, Tower Ballroom.

27 January 1962
Liverpool-Aintree, Aintree Institute.
Last concert at Aintree Institute.

28 January 1962
Liverpool-West Derby,
Casbah Coffee Club.

29 January 1962
Southport, Kingsway Club.

30 and 31 January 1962
Liverpool, Cavern Club.

The hundreds of shows
performed under difficult
conditions, as seen in this series
of shots, became the Beatles'
"training ground".

1 February 1962
Afternoon
Liverpool, Cavern Club.
Evening
West Kirby, Thistle Café.
Performance without John Lennon.
With Steve Day & the Drifters.

2 February 1962
Manchester, Oasis Club.
With the Allan Dent Jazz Band.

3 February 1962
Liverpool, Cavern Club.
With Gerry & the Pacemakers,
the Saints Jazz Band.

4 February 1962
Liverpool-West Derby, Casbah Coffee Club.

**The Beatles by now were
pleasantly assailed by hundreds
of girls who would do anything to
be "close" to their sweethearts.**

5 February 1962
Afternoon
Liverpool, Cavern Club.
Evening
Southport, Kingsway Club.
With the Quiet Ones.
(For this show, Ringo Starr replaced
ailing Pete Best on drums.)

7 February 1962
Liverpool, Cavern Club.

9 February 1962
Afternoon
Liverpool, Cavern Club.
Evening
Liverpool, Cavern Club.
Birkenhead, Technical College Hall.

10 February 1962
Birkenhead-Tranmere.
St. Paul's Presbyterian Church Hall Youth Club.

11 February 1962
Liverpool-West Derby, Casbah Coffee Club.

12 February 1962
Manchester, BBC Radio.
The Beatles' first recording for the BBC,
arranged by Epstein, on 10 January when
they played four songs:
Like Dreamers Do, *Till There Was You*, *Memphis
Tennessee* and *Hello Little Girl*
The band was deemed suitable to perform for
the teen radio show "Teenager's Turn".
On 20 February a contract was signed that set
the recording of the show for 7 March.

13 and 14 February 1962
Liverpool, Cavern Club.

15 February 1962
Afternoon
Liverpool, Cavern Club.
Evening
New Brighton, Tower Ballroom.
With Terry Lightfoot & His New Orleans
Jazz Band.

16 February 1962
Birkenhead, Technical College Hall.

New Brighton, Tower Ballroom

17 February 1962
Liverpool, Cavern Club.

18 February 1962
Liverpool-West Derby, Casbah Coffee Club.

19 February 1962
Liverpool, Cavern Club.

20 February 1962
Southport, Floral Hall.
With Gerry & the Pacemakers, Rory Storm &
the Hurricanes, the Chris Hamilton Jazzmen.

21 February 1962
Liverpool, Cavern Club.

23 February 1962
Afternoon
Liverpool, Cavern Club.
Evening
New Brighton, Tower Ballroom.
Birkenhead, Technical College Hall.

24 February 1962
Evening
Hoylake, YMCA.
From midnight
Liverpool, Cavern Club.
With the Red River Jazzmen, Tom Smith's
Jazzmen, the Vintage.

25 February 1962
Liverpool-West Derby, Casbah Coffee Club.

26 February 1962
Southport, Kingsway Club.

27 February 1962
Liverpool, Cavern Club.

28 February 1962
Liverpool, Cavern Club.
With Gerry & the Pacemakers,
Johnny Sandon & the Searchers.

1 March 1962
Afternoon
Liverpool, Cavern Club.
Evening
Liverpool, Storyville Jazz Club.

2 March 1962
Bootle, St. John's Hall.
With Johnny Sandon's Searchers, the Teenbeats.

New Brighton, Tower Ballroom.

3 March 1962
Liverpool, Cavern Club.
With Jim McHarg's Jazzmen.

4 March 1962
Liverpool-West Derby, Casbah Coffee Club.

5 March 1962
Afternoon
Liverpool, Cavern Club.
Evening
Southport, Kingsway Club.

6 March 1962
Liverpool, Cavern Club.

7 March 1962
Playhouse Theatre, St. John's Rd., Manchester.
Recording for the radio show "Teenager's Turn".
3:45 pm
Rehearsal.
8:00 pm – 8:45 pm
Live recording before an audience.
The Beatles played four songs, three of which
were broadcast the next day:
Hello Little Girl (cut)
Dream Baby (1:50)
Memphis Tennessee (2:15)
Please Mr. Postman (2:00)

8 March 1962
BBC Radio, "Teenager's Turn".
The show recorded the previous
day was broadcast.
Presenter: Ray Peters
Producer: Peter Pilbeam
With the Northern Dance Orchestra,
Trad Lads, Brad Newman:
Dream Baby (1:50)
Memphis Tennessee (2:15)
Please Mr. Postman (2:00)

Liverpool, Storyville Jazz Club.

9 March 1962
Liverpool, Cavern Club.

10 March 1962
Birkenhead-Tranmere.
St. Paul's Presbyterian Church Hall Youth Club.
With the Country Four and Brian Newman.

11 March 1962
Liverpool-West Derby, Casbah Coffee Club.

12 March 1962
Southport, Kingsway Club.

17 March 1962.
The poster of the concert
at Knotty Ash Hall
for Saint Patrick's Day.

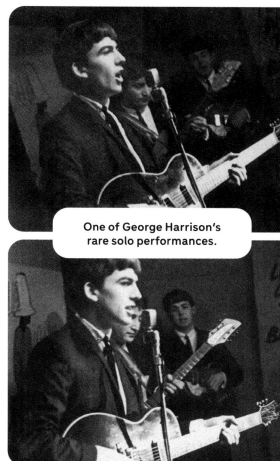

One of George Harrison's
rare solo performances.

13 e 14 March 1962
Liverpool, Cavern Club.

15 March 1962
Afternoon
Liverpool, Cavern Club.
Evening
Liverpool, Storyville Jazz Club.

16 March 1962
Liverpool, Cavern Club.

17 March 1962
Liverpool-Knotty Ash, Village Hall.
With Rory Storm & the Hurricanes.

18 March 1962
Liverpool-West Derby, Casbah Coffee Club.

19 March 1962
Southport, Kingsway Club.

20, 21 and 22 March 1962
Liverpool, Cavern Club.

23 March 1962
Afternoon
Liverpool, Cavern Club.
Evening
Liverpool, Cavern Club.
With Gerry & the Pacemakers.

24 March 1962
Heswall, Barnston Women's Institute, Heswall
Jazz Club (first performance in which the Beatles
appeared in suits and ties bought by Brian.
These had only previously been used for the BBC
recording). With the Pasadena Jazzmen.

25 March 1962
Liverpool-West Derby, Casbah Coffee Club.

26 March 1962
Liverpool, Cavern Club.

28 March 1962
Afternoon
Liverpool, Cavern Club.
Evening
Liverpool, Cavern Club.
With Gerry & the Pacemakers,
the Remo Four.

29 March 1962
Liverpool, Odd Spot Club.
With the Mersey Beats.

30 March 1962
Afternoon
Liverpool, Cavern Club.
Evening
Liverpool, Cavern Club.
With the Dallas Jazz Band.

31 March 1962
Stroud, Subscription Rooms.
With the Rebel Rousers.

Here and on opposite page:
**Yes, they had given up wearing black leather, but definitely
not the habit of joking around onstage. Brian Epstein
disapproved, since he wanted them to be
"clean and professional".**

1 April 1962
Liverpool-West Derby, Casbah Coffee Club.

2 April 1962
Afternoon
Liverpool, Cavern Club.
Evening
Liverpool, Pavilion Theatre.
With the Royal Waterford Showband.

4 April 1962
Afternoon
Liverpool, Cavern Club.
Evening
Liverpool, Cavern Club.
With the Dominoes, the Four Jays.

5 April 1962
Liverpool, Cavern Club. Evening for their fan
club "the Beatles for Their Fans or An Evening
with George, John, Paul and Pete".
With the Four Jays.

6 April 1962
Afternoon
Liverpool, Cavern Club.
Evening
New Brighton, Tower Ballroom.
With Emile Ford & the Checkmates, Gerry & the
Pacemakers, Howie Casey & the Seniors, Rory
Storm & the Hurricanes, the Big Three,
the Original King Twisters.

7 April 1962
Liverpool-West Derby, Casbah Coffee Club.

Liverpool, Cavern Club.
With the Saints Jazz Band.
(Performance without George Harrison
who was ill.)

8 April 1962
Liverpool-West Derby, Casbah Coffee Club.
(Performance without George Harrison
who was ill.)

13 April 1962. The Beatles performed at the Star-Club in Hamburg with Roy Young on piano.

On 10 April Stuart Sutcliffe died in Hamburg of a cerebral haemorrhage.

The Beatles, particularly John, were deeply affected by his death. Lennon, McCartney and Best arrived in Hamburg on 11 April. They were joined the next day by Epstein and Harrison (George had been ill and his arrival had been delayed).

They were playing in a new venue, the Star-Club, owned by Manfred Weissleder. With the ways of a gangster, he was a newcomer to the business. Weissleder, who had only recently opened the club, had booked the Beatles in late January in Liverpool. He had made the trip there to scout for bands for the new club. He was accompanied by Horst Fascher, a former bouncer at the Kaiserkeller and Top Ten.

April–May 1962. German tour poster and rare color photo.

The Beatles, with a contract in hand for 500 DM each per week, set off on their new adventure. While in Hamburg, Epstein negotiated the termination of the contract that bound the Beatles to Polydor. To obtain this, he agreed to a final recording session for Polydor during which two songs were recorded: *Sweet Georgia Brown* and *Swanee River*.

Lewisohn traces these sessions to sometime between 23 and 27 April, though without any details as to where the recordings took place. A schedule from the Polydor Rahlstadt studios in Hamburg, however, proves that the recordings were made on 24 May 1962 (Paul McCartney is indicated as arranger for *Sweet Georgia Brown*). The lineup at the studio for these recordings was:

John Lennon	–	Electric Guitar / Voice
Paul McCartney	–	Bass / Voice
George Harrison	–	Electric Guitar / Voice
Pete Best	–	Drums
Roy Young	–	Piano

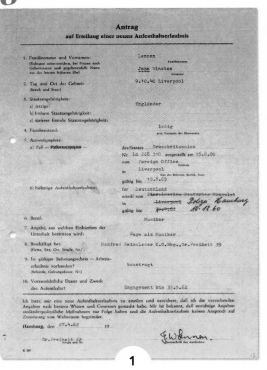

1

2

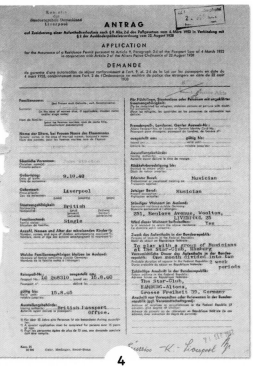

4

5

Antrag

auf Erteilung eines Sichtvermerks zur Einreise nach — zur Durchreise durch — Deutschland
Application for a Visa to enter — to travel through — Germany
Demande de délivrance d'un visa d'entrée en — de transit par — l'Allemagne

An d.... Botschaft — Gesandtschaft — Generalkonsulat der Bundesrepublik Deutschland
To the Embassy — Legation — Consulate-General of the Federal Republic of Germany
Ambassade — Légation — Consulat Général de la République fédérale d'Allemagne

in / in / à

1. Familien- und Vornamen	Lennon
Surname and Christian names	
Nom de famille et prénoms	John Winston

2. Geburtstag und Geburtsort	geboren am 9.10.40
Date and place of birth	in Liverpool, England
Date et lieu de naissance	

| 3. Wohnsitz oder dauernder Aufenthaltsort | 251, Menlove Avenue, Woolton, Liverpool 25. |

Domicile: 12-14, Whitechapel, Liverpool 1

Entry Visa

| 4. Familienstand | ledig Single |
| Marital Status | |

| 5. Staatsangehörigkeit | jetzige British |
| Nationality | |

| 6. Beruf | Musician. |
| Trade or profession | 30th August 1962 |

3

Antrag   LENNON
auf Erteilung einer neuen Aufenthaltserlaubnis

1. Familienname und Vornamen: LENNON (JOHN WINSTON)
   JA JOHN WINSTON

2. Tag und Ort der Geburt: 9th Oct 1940 LIVERPOOL

3. Staatsangehörigkeit:
   a) jetzige: BRITISH
   b) frühere Staatsangehörigkeit: BRITISH
   c) weitere fremde Staatsangehörigkeit: KEINE

4. Familienstand:

5. Ausweispapiere:
   a) Paß – Paßersatzpapier –   des Staates GT BRITAIN
      Nr.60 36530 ausgestellt am 15 AG 1900
      von FOREIGN OFFICE
      in LIVERPOOL
      gültig bis 15th AUG 1965

   b) bisherige Aufenthaltserlaubnis:

6. Beruf: MUSICIAN

7. Angabe, aus welchen Einkünften der Unterhalt bestritten wird: SALARY

8. Beschäftigt bei: MANFRED WEISSLEDER K.S

9. Ist gültiger Befreiungsschein – Arbeitserlaubnis vorhanden?

10. Voraussichtliche Dauer und Zweck des Aufenthalts?   1ST NOU — 15th NOV–18 DEC –2nd JAN

Ich bitte, mir eine neue Aufenthaltserlaubnis zu erteilen und versichere, daß ich die vorstehenden Angaben nach bestem Wissen und Gewissen gemacht habe. Mir ist bekannt, daß unrichtige Angaben ausländerpolizeiliche Maßnahmen zur Folge haben und die Aufenthaltserlaubnis keinen Anspruch auf Zuweisung von Wohnraum begründen.

Hamburg, den 14th NOV R 1962.
GROSSE FREIHEIT 39

6

Tony Sheridan (vocalist) overdubbed the song in a session on 7 June 1962.

Here are the details of the band's activity in Hamburg during that period:

13 April – 31 May 1962
Hamburg-St. Pauli, Star-Club.
48 Evenings (20 April day off).

From Monday to Friday
8:00 pm – 2:00 am
Saturday
8:00 pm – 4:00 am
Sunday
8:00 pm – 2:00 am
With Tex Roberg, Roy Young, the Graduates, the Bachelors. In April, also, with Little Richard, and in May with Gene Vincent, the Tony Sheridan Quartet, Gerry & the Pacemakers.

1, 2, 3, 4, 5 and 6.
John Lennon's requests for residence and work permits for the period he was engaged at the Star-Club in Hamburg.

Ringo arrives, "Love me do" is released

Back home again, the Beatles spent 3 June rehearsing at the Cavern behind closed doors to prepare for an important appointment on 6 June... On 5 October 1962 the single *Love Me Do/P.S. I Love You* was put on sale at music stores.

But wait a minute, you are wondering, 'and the 6 June appointment?' Yes precisely. Let us take a moment to back track four months from that 5 October date. It in fact marked the final act of a story that had begun one fateful 6 June of the same year. It was 6:00 pm at 3 Abbey Road, London, NW8. Since 1931, this had been the premises of the EMI recording studios, formerly Gramophone Company Limited.

The EMI recording studios at Abbey Road deserve a short digression for their fundamental importance in the history of music (see Frame pp. 92-93). In this veritable inner sanctum imbued with an almost saintly aura, the first fortunate person to have "sighted" the Beatles upon their arrival at the studios was John Skinner, the guard. Skinner later related: "The Beatles pulled into the car park in an old white van. They all looked very thin and weedy, almost under-nourished. Neil Aspinall, their road manager, said that they were the Beatles, here for a session. I thought what a strange name!".

Those present at the Beatles' 6 June recording session were George Martin, Ron Richards, Norman Smith, and Chris Neal, all of whom with great consternation found themselves faced with these four rather scruffy "provincials". The boys were dressed in black leather and jeans, and their equipment was absolutely "indescribable", as the fussy technical personnel at Abbey Road in their white coats described the scene.

The record cover of the mythic *Love Me Do*.

**The Beatles during rehearsals at the Cavern Club
on one of their countless working afternoons
in 1962, between afternoon and evening shows.**

George Martin even had to explain to the band how to use the studio microphones. Once they were ready to record (they were in fact not going to make a commercial recording, but just a demo to give Martin a chance to see if anything good could be made out of it all), the Beatles played four songs: *Besame Mucho*, *Love Me Do*, *P.S. I Love You*, and *Ask Me Why*.

While they were playing *Love Me Do* Smith asked Neal to go get George from the bar and see what he thought of it. Despite the keen interest the band seemed to have sparked in Martin, in the end he simply remarked, "We have nothing to lose" and signed them with a standard recording contract. He was careful to have it backdated to 4 June, to ensure EMI rights on the recordings just made. The second episode of this event unfolded on 4 September of the same year.

Three months after the Beatles first stepped into the studios at Abbey Road, they returned, but this second time they took a flight from Liverpool, stayed in a hotel in Chelsea, and arrived at the studios after lunch "to make history". In the meantime, they had shamelessly dropped Pete Best and replaced him with Ringo Starr, who had been the drummer with Rory Storm & the Hurricanes. The true story of how Pete Best was replaced became one of the pages of their story that

[Contd., p. 94] ⟶

The EMI recording studios at 3 Abbey Road, St. John's Wood, are today world famous as being where almost all of the Beatles' recordings were made from 1962 to 1970. The studios in fact were officially rebaptized "Abbey Road Studios" reflecting the international renown they had received after the Fab Four's album of the same name was released. Since then, the pedestrian crossing and the entrance to the studios, just a few meters away, have become truly iconic for all Beatles fans. The history of the Studios before the Beatles, however, was no less glorious. There had been an impressive number of great artists who had recorded there, and "sanctified" the Studios.

The Vice President of EMI Studios, Martin Benge, explained that over the years the wall surrounding the Studio grounds had become several centimetres thicker due to the repeated coats of paint needed to cover up the writings left by fans from the entire world.

The history of the studios at Abbey Road began in 1927 when Captain Osmond "Ozzy" Williams decided to fulfil his dream as a youth and create a recording studio in northeast London. Unfortunately the Captain died before he could finish the project.

EMI, the historic owner of the studios, was founded in 1897 as "the Gramophone Company". Two years later, in London, the Company bought the painting entitled "His Master's Voice" by Francis Barraud. The image of the painting, the famous puppy "Nipper", as well as the painting's name became its trademark. It is still in use today as one of EMI's labels, HMV (His Master's Voice). By 1912 the Company had factories in eight countries, including Britain and Russia, and sales offices in twelve countries. Based on a survey during the period it was estimated that a third of British households had a gramophone (most of them were the brand HMV of course). In 1921 the first HMV store was inaugurated, on Oxford Street, by English composer Sir Edward Elgar.

Historically, the first recording session in the new studios, then called HMV Studios, took place during November 1931. The Gramophone Company (precisely the year it changed its name to EMI – Electric and Musical Industries) spent £100,000 for the acquisition of one of the most sophisticated recording studios of its time. Most importantly, it was the world's first structure designed and built uniquely for the purpose of recording. The Company then asked the great Sir Edward Elgar (Broadheat, Worcester 1857-Worcester 1934) to conduct (and record) the London Symphony Orchestra in a performance of *Land of Hope and Glory* (footage also exists of this session).

The following year, Elgar also directed the then sixteen-year-old violinist Yehudi Menuhin (New York 1912-Berlin 1999). The young musician was destined to be lauded as one of the world's greatest violinists. The recording of *Violin Concerto* remains one of the most outstanding recordings of all times. Sir Edward Elgar, often considered the "father of twentieth-century English music", was knighted and received membership in the Order of Merit in 1911. He received the title of "Master of the King's Music" in 1924, as well as Baronet by King George V. History often remembers Sir Elgar when, in 1933, even as he lay gravely ill and bedridden, he directed the rehearsal of his *Caractacus* taking place at the studios at Abbey Road. This was made possible by an innovative telephone connection.

Since then, some veritable milestone performances in classical music have been recorded in these studios (and in recent years remastered by a process that has adopted the name Abbey Road Technology). During WWII, the studios remained open and Glenn Miller recorded his last performance in 1944 at Abbey Road. A band member, Nat Peck, recalled that the recording was meant to be used for propaganda purposes. Glenn Miller spoke in German, and the recording was then broadcast in Germany.

Before the Beatles, other pop stars had come to Abbey Road to record. There Cliff Richard with the Drifters (later the Shadows), for example, made his first single *Move It*. Yet if there was one pop music figure to be associated with the studios at Abbey Road, it could be no other than Sir George Martin. He began working with the studios in 1950, after leaving Parlophone's Classical section. In 1955, Martin became manager of the label and began producing his first "comedy" records with Beyond the Fringe and Peter Sellers.

There have been tons written about the Beatles' first visit on 6 June 1962, yet there were also other legendary artists whose sounds reverberated within the walls of the studios. There was the Pink Floyd that, apart from the Beatles, were the first to introduce a series of night recording sessions at Abbey Road (the studios normally closed at 10:00 pm). The Pink Floyd recorded their masterpiece *Dark Side of the Moon* at the Studios, among other albums. They were one of the bands to leave "bad memories" with the studio staff. Manager Alan Stagge related that the only way to kick them out at night, or rather late the next morning, was to burst into the studio and switch off the electricity…

Another "mythic" recording of the sixties featured Cilla Black and her *Alfie* in Studio 1. The song was produced by George Martin, with the orchestral arrangement by Burt Bacharach. Cilla insisted that the only way she could record the song was under the condition that Bacharach came from the U.S. to London. In addition, she wanted him to be the arranger, and also personally play in the recording. It seemed an impossible demand, and a pretext not to record the song, but Martin called Bacharach anyway to try to persuade him. Martin assured him that it would be good by Take 3 at the most. And, of course, as promised, on Take 3 they had their recording, and the song was released.

Other historic recordings were the soundtracks of *Return of the Jedi* and *Raiders of the Lost Ark* (in addition to the last of the Trilogy of *the Lord of the Rings* and the first two of the *Harry Potter* films).

The history of Abbey Road is a fantastic saga. It is inextricably linked to the history of music. This was well expressed by George Martin who reflected that if we believed, as he did, that a house could have an atmosphere capable of absorbing the personalities and feelings of its inhabitants, then we would not have any difficulty in appreciating the unique gifts of Abbey Road. Paul McCartney expressed his feelings for Abbey Road, explaining that he loved it because it had depth, a history, a tradition… He thought that Abbey Road was the best studio in the city, of a city that was the world.

John Lennon at the Cavern Club performs on the classical guitar. Paul McCartney, with back turned, accompanies him on the bass.

at the time remained buried in the band's secret archives. Indeed it was enacted in such a cowardly way and was nothing to be proud of.

George Martin was waiting for them with the song *How Do You Do It* that he felt was "right" for them. The Beatles did not share his feeling though, and in fact they recorded a version of the song that was completely bland and lifeless. They wanted to do something of their own, they told Martin. If they were capable of writing something just as good, Martin had replied, then they were free to do so.

Just for the records, *How Do You Do It* was recorded by another Liverpool

band, Gerry and the Pacemakers. They were also managed by Brian Epstein and recorded the song in just one take. When it was released, it shot straight to the top of the charts.

As for the Beatles, after their little "rebellion" they went out for some spaghetti at 3 schillings and 6 pences at the Alpino, a restaurant on Marylebone High Street (the establishment thus earned its three seconds of limelight in the history of music). The Beatles went back to the studios and recorded *Love Me Do*. After grumbling, protests and retakes, the recording was finally completed around 10:00 pm.

Among the most adamant grumblers was Martin himself. He did not find the session of 4 September convincing at all, and he particularly had real doubts about Ringo on drums. And so he decided to hire the services of a studio session drummer, the thirty-two-year-old Andy White, who was a much more mature and experienced musician.

Poor Ringo, dethroned after just one session. He was relegated to playing a tambourine for the second recording on 11 September, with White on drums. Today, to distinguish between the two versions of *Love Me Do*, all we have to do is listen for the tambourine. If we hear it, it is the 11 September version with White on drums. If there is no tambourine, then it is the version with Ringo as drummer.

During that same session, the Beatles also recorded *P.S. I Love You*, with again White on drums. They then attempted a version of *Please Please Me*, though they soon gave it up until a better moment.

Finally, on 5 October came the release of *Love Me Do / P.S. I Love You* (Parlophone 45-R 4949). The most impassioned Beatlemaniacs all know that the first cut of the single was the 4 September version with Ringo on drums. All of the copies from 1963, including those right up to today, are the 11 September version. The switch happened with the release of *The Beatles Hits Extended Play*.

For some obscure reason, it was decided to use the version with White on drums for the EP. Moreover, it was also decided that all future copies of *Love Me Do* be made from that master. To avoid any confusion, in a shining example of EMI's efficiency, the master with Ringo... was destroyed!

The single *Love Me Do* reached seventeenth on the charts, with sales largely concentrated in Liverpool. This made some journalists suspect that maybe Epstein himself had bought a large quantity (10,000). Brian always denied this, but his associates and the Beatles themselves admitted this was highly likely. In this regard, John Lennon's reply to a journalist might give us a clue. When a journalist asked him how it was that with a record on the charts, John still had to be so careful about how much he spent on meals, John apparently remarked that "someone has to pay for all of those damned copies of *Love Me Do*".

It is left up to journalists, history, or myth to decide what to believe. Paul McCartney, during a BBC interview in 1989, was specifically asked about this question and the recording session:

D. **What do you remember about having to record *Love Me Do* with Andy White, the session drummer?**
R. Well, George Martin didn't think that Ringo was a very good drummer. On all these Lita Roza, Alma Cogan records that were in vogue shortly before us, the drummers were pretty good show drummers, so producers were used to

In the detail of the bass drum, we note the old
Beatles logo, with a beetle's antennae sticking
out of the "B" of Beatles.

hearing a bass drum in the right place, locking in with the bass guitar like it would now. We weren't really bothered with that. Ours was very four in the bar — boom, boom, boom, boom — we used to try and break stages with it. That's what eventually got called the Mersey Beat. So Andy White was the kind of professional drummer that we weren't really used to, and George obviously thought that Ringo was a little bit out of time, a little bit unsteady on tempo. We never really had to be steady on tempo. We liked to be but it didn't matter if we slowed down or went faster, because we all went at the same time. So that was a major disappointment for Ringo.

When we *first* came down in June 1962, with Pete Best, George took us aside and said "I'm not happy about the drummer". And we all went, "Oh God, well I'm not telling him. You tell him... Oh God!" and it was quite a blow. He said "Can you change your drummer?" and we said "Well,we're quite happy with him, he works great in the clubs". And George said "Yes, but for recording he's got to be just a bit more accurate". Pete had never quite been like the rest of us. We were the wacky trio and Pete was perhaps a little more... sensible; he was slightly different from us, he wasn't quite as artsy as we were. And we just didn't hang out that much together. He'd go home to his Mum's club, the Casbah, and although we'd hang out there with him, we never really went to other places together. So then we changed to Ringo, who'd been with Rory Storm and the Hurricanes, went back to London and found that George didn't even like him! We said, "But you're kidding! This is the best drummer in Liverpool, this guy, he's out of Rory Storm and the Hurricanes! This is class!". And George went, [eyes to the ceiling, stifling a yawn] "Oh yes? Well, I still like Andy White!". So then Ringo got to play tambourine instead, which was very humiliating for him. God knows how he must have been brought down — you never can be in someone else's head.

I actually remember a lot of those early sessions. When we first came to the studio to do *Love Me Do*, Dezo Hoffmann, the photographer, was there to take some shots for black-and-white handout photos which we needed. George [Harrison] always hated those because he had a black eye. He'd been bopped in the Cavern by some guy who was jealous over his girlfriend! Anyway, we got on with *Love Me Do*. We started playing it, [singing] "Love, love me do / you know I love you" and I'm singing harmony then it gets to the "pleeeaase". STOP. John goes "Love me..." and then put his harmonica to his mouth: "Wah, wah, wahhh". George Martin went "Wait a minute, wait a minute, there's a crossover there. Someone else has got to sing 'Love Me Do' because you can't go 'Love Me waahhh'. You're going to have a song called 'Love me waahh'! So, Paul, will you sing 'Love Me Do'!".

God, I got the screaming heebe-geebies. I mean he suddenly changed this whole arrangement that we'd been doing forever, and John was to miss out that line: he'd sing "Pleeeeease", put his mouth-organ to his mouth, I'd sing "Love Me Do" and John would come in "Waahhh wahhhh wahhhhhh". We we're doing it live, there was no real overdubbing, so I was suddenly given this massive moment, on our first record, no backing, where everything stopped, the spotlight was on me and I went [in shaky singing voice] "Love me doooo". And I can still hear the shake in my voice when I listen to that record! I was terrified. When we went back up to Liverpool I remember talking to Johnny Gustafson of the Big Three and he said "You should have let John sing that line"! John did sing it better than me, he had a lower voice and was a little more bluesy at singing that line.

I also remember those great big white studio sight-screens, like at a cricket match, towering over you. And up this endless stairway was the control room.

It was like heaven, where the great Gods lived, and we were down below. Oh God, the nerves! Anyway, it worked out well and from then on we started to get a bit more confidence. So much so that ultimately we started to see what recording was about. George [Martin] was very, very helpful in the early days, he was the mastermind then. But as it went on the workers took over the tools more, and we started to say "We're coming in late, and we might not need you, George. If you can't make it, we'll go in on our own".

(Source: Lewisohn, 1988, 6)

Although the Beatles were busy "making history", they nevertheless continued performing at their usual relentless pace during the period from the beginning of June until end-October. The details of these engagements are as follows:

9 June 1962
Liverpool, Cavern Club.
Beatles Welcome Home Show.
With the Red River Jazzmen, Ken Dallas & the Silhouettes, the Four Jays.

11 June 1962
BBC Radio.
Playhouse Theatre, St. John's Rd., Manchester.
Live performance broadcast 15 June
"Here We Go (Beatles in Concert)".

12 and 13 June 1962
Liverpool, Cavern Club.

15 June 1962
BBC Radio.
"Here We Go (Beatles in Concert)".
Presenter: Ray Peters
Producer: Peter Pilbeam
Ask Me Why (2:13)
Besame Mucho (2:24)
A Picture of You (2:11)

Afternoon
Liverpool, Cavern Club.
Evening
Liverpool, Cavern Club.
With the Spidermen.

16 June 1962
Liverpool, Cavern Club.
With Tony Smith's Jazzmen.

19 June 1962
Afternoon
Liverpool, Cavern Club.
Evening
Liverpool, Cavern Club.
With the Bluegenes, Ken Dallas & the Silhouettes.

20 June 1962
Afternoon
Liverpool, Cavern Club.
Evening
Liverpool, Cavern Club.
With the Sorrals, the Strangers.

21 June 1962
New Brighton, Tower Ballroom.
With Bruce Channel, the Barons & Delbert
McLinton, the Statesmen, the Big Three,
the Four Jays.

22 June 1962
Afternoon
Liverpool, Cavern Club.
Evening
Liverpool, Cavern Club.
With the Cyclones.

23 June 1962
Northwich, Victory Memorial Hall.

24 June 1962
Liverpool-West Derby, Casbah Coffee Club.

25 June 1962
Afternoon
Liverpool, Cavern Club.
Evening
St. Helens, Plaza Ballroom.
With the Big Three.

27 June 1962
Afternoon
Liverpool, Cavern Club.
Evening
Liverpool, Cavern Club.
With the Big Three.

28 June 1962
Birkenhead, Majestic Ballroom.

29 June 1962
Afternoon
Liverpool, Cavern Club.
Evening
New Brighton, Tower Ballroom.
Operation Big Beat III.
Performance by the Beatles and nine bands.

30 June 1962
Heswall, Barnston Women's Institute,
Heswall Jazz Club.
With the Big Three.

1 July 1962
Liverpool, Cavern Club.
With Gene Vincent,
the Bluegenes, the Sounds Incorporated.
The Beatles played as backing band for Gene
Vincent in *What'd I Say.*

2 July 1962
St. Helens, Plaza Ballroom.

3 and 4 July 1962
Liverpool, Cavern Club.

5 July 1962
Birkenhead, Majestic Ballroom.

6 July 1962
Mersey River, show onboard
the boat "Royal Iris".
With Mr. Acker Bilk's Paramount Jazz Band.

7 July 1962
Birkenhead-Port Sunlight, Hulme Hall.

8 July 1962
Liverpool, Cavern Club.

9 July 1962
St. Helens, Plaza Ballroom.

10 and 11 July 1962
Liverpool, Cavern Club.

12 July 1962
Afternoon
Liverpool, Cavern Club.
Evening
Birkenhead, Majestic Ballroom.

13 July 1962
New Brighton, Tower Ballroom.

14 July 1962
Rhyl, Regent Dansette.
With the Strangers.

15 July 1962
Liverpool, Cavern Club.

16 July 1962
Afternoon
Liverpool, Cavern Club.
Evening
St. Helens, Plaza Ballroom.

17 July 1962
Swindon, McIlroy's Ballroom.

18 July 1962
Liverpool, Cavern Club.

19 July 1962
Birkenhead, Majestic Ballroom.

20 July 1962
Liverpool, Cavern Club.

21 July 1962
New Brighton, Tower Ballroom.

22 July 1962
Liverpool, Cavern Club.

23 July 1962
Southport, Kingsway Club.

24 July 1962
Liverpool, Cavern Club.

25 July 1962
Afternoon
Liverpool, Cavern Club.
Evening
Liverpool, Cavern Club.

26 July 1962
Southport, Cambridge Hall.
With Joe Brown & His Bruvvers.

27 July 1962
New Brighton, Tower Ballroom.
With Joe Brown & His Bruvvers, the Big Three,
the Four Jays, the Statesmen,
Steve Day & the Drifters.

The hour of Pete Best's demise was approaching. Pete played on 15 August for the last time with the Beatles in two shows (afternoon and evening) at the Cavern Club. On 16 and 17 August he was temporarily replaced on drums by Johnny Hutchinson who was then with the Big Three. This was the same drummer who, being a member of the Cassanovas band, had accompanied the Beatles during part of the audition for Larry Parnes on 10 May 1961.

On 18 August, Ringo Starr definitively claimed his place as drummer of the Beatles during the show at Hulme Hall in Birkenhead.

As mentioned, the dismissal of Pete Best and the arrival of Ringo Starr became one of the most controversial issues in the history of the band. For years, rumour after rumour fuelled speculation on the reasons for Pete's dismissal. The only thing for sure was that Brian Epstein on Thursday 16 August 1962 coldly informed Pete that the Beatles had decided to replace him with Ringo Starr. Ringo at the time was playing with Rory Storm & the Hurricanes. Fans took revenge by beating up George and seriously threatening Brian, who for a while avoided going to the Cavern. Yet, poor Pete was marked forever by this event (that seemed to confirm what John Lennon declared many years later about the rest of the Beatles, that they were the "greatest bastards on earth").

Best continued playing on the music circuit and also found a job at the Liverpool employment agency. These were hard years for him, though in the mid-nineties he did receive a very big amount of money in royalties. These were for some songs released on the album *Anthology 1*, on which Best had been drummer.

At the time, it was said that Pete had received approximately 9 million Euros, though he himself never confirmed this. If this were true however, there is no doubt that these monies would have represented a more than well deserved compensation for his brutal dismissal more than thirty years previously.

The last photos of Pete Best while he was with the Beatles. He was shortly to be replaced by Ringo Starr.

22 August 1962. Ringo Starr is seen with a tuft of prematurely greying hair. A short while later, following Brian's advice, Ringo started to tint his hair.

28 July 1962
Evening
Birkenhead, Majestic Ballroom.
Mersey Beat Ball. With the Bluegenes,
Billy Kramer & the Coasters.
From midnight
Liverpool, Cavern Club. With Dee Fenton
& the Silhouettes, the Red River Jazzmen.

30 July 1962
Afternoon
Liverpool, Cavern Club.

Evening
Bootle, St. John's Hall, Blue Penguin Club.

1 August 1962
Afternoon
Liverpool, Cavern Club.
Evening
Liverpool, Cavern Club.
With Gerry & the Pacemakers,
the Mersey Beats.

22 August 1962. On these pages a series of shots of the Beatles rehearsing for their performance on Granada TV. Also in this series of photos, the first of Ringo Starr on drums with the Beatles.

3 August 1962
Liverpool, Grafton Rooms.
With Gerry & the Pacemakers, the Big Three.
The Beatles played:
Some Other Guy
Shimmy Shimmy (I Do)
Darktown Strutters' Ball
Love Me Do
Ain't She Sweet
Don't Ever Change
Hey Baby
Soldier of Love (Lay Down Your Arms)
A Picture of You
Falling in Love Again (Can't Help It)
A Shot of Rhythm and Blues
Sharing You
I Remember You
Mr. Moonlight
P.S. I Love You
Please Mr. Postman
Red Hot
Besame Mucho

4 August 1962
Higher Bebington, Victoria Hall.

5 August 1962
Liverpool, Cavern Club.
With the Saints Jazz Band.

7 August 1962
Afternoon
Liverpool, Cavern Club.
Evening
Liverpool, Cavern Club.
With the Swinging Bluegenes, Ken Dallas &
the Silhouettes, Wayne Stephens & the Vikings.

8 August 1962
Doncaster, Co-op Ballroom.

9 August 1962
Liverpool, Cavern Club.

10 August 1962
Mersey River, show onboard
the boat "Royal Iris".
With Johnny Kidd & the Pirates, the Dakotas.

11 August 1962
Liverpool, Odd Spot Club.

12 August 1962
Liverpool, Cavern Club.

13 August 1962
Afternoon
Liverpool, Cavern Club.
Evening
Crewe, Majestic Ballroom.

15 August 1962
Afternoon
Liverpool, Cavern Club.
Evening
Liverpool, Cavern Club
(last performance with Pete Best).

Temporary change in lineup since Ringo was
not available to replace Pete before 18 August,
and understandably, Pete was not available to
stay on for another two days.

THE BEATLES
**(John Lennon, Paul McCartney, George
Harrison, Johnny Hutchinson)**

16 August 1962
Chester, Riverpark Ballroom.

17 August 1962
Birkenhead, Majestic Ballroom.

New Brighton, Tower Ballroom.

THE BEATLES
(John Lennon, Paul McCartney, George Harrison, Ringo Starr)

18 August 1962
Birkenhead-Port Sunlight, Hulme Hall.
The Beatles performed here with the lineup
that would remain unchanged
until the group broke up.

19 August 1962
Liverpool, Cavern Club

20 August 1962
Crewe, Majestic Ballroom.

22 August 1962
The first performance of the Beatles before TV
cameras. Granada Television filmed them at the
Cavern for the 17 October 1962 show "People
and Places". There was a rebroadcast on 6
November 1963 for the program "Scene at 6:30"
of *Some Other Guy* only.

**A smiling George Harrison
rehearses before going onstage to be
filmed by Granada TV.**

The songs below were recorded on 22 August:
Some Other Guy
Kansas City / Hey-Hey-Hey-Hey!

23 August 1962
Chester, Riverpark Ballroom.

The date of 23 August 1962 also marked John Lennon's marriage to Miss Cynthia Powell. Though it may seem strange that a newly wed groom spends the first night of his honeymoon performing with his band in a club instead of being with his bride, this was precisely what happened (also because apparently the groom had already spent nights with his new wife before, since Cynthia was already expecting a child when they were married). The best men were Paul and Brian, and the maid of honour was Marjorie Joyce Powell (Cynthia's sister-in-law). George also attended. John and Cynthia were joined in marriage at the Liverpool Mount Pleasant Register Office, to the deafening roar of a hammer drill outside in the street. No one could hear a thing...!

24 August 1962
Afternoon
Liverpool, Cavern Club.
Evening
Birkenhead, Majestic Ballroom.

25 August 1962
Fleetwood, Marine Hall Ballroom.

26 August 1962
Liverpool, Cavern Club. With Mike Berry.

Above: **30 July 1962. The poster for the show at the Blue Penguin Club.**
Below: **17 August 1962. The poster for the Beatles' show at the Tower Ballroom.**

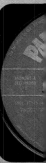

All of the editions, promotional or not, of the first press of *Love Me Do*. Each one is different, although in some cases only because of a minute detail that only a collector's eye could catch.

Above: **14 September 1962. The Beatles performed at the Tower Ballroom with other bands.** Below: **25 September 1962. The poster for the concert at Heswall Jazz Club.**

28 August 1962
Liverpool, Cavern Club.
With the Bluegenes, Gerry Levine & the Avengers.

29 August 1962
Morecambe, Floral Hall Ballroom.

30 August 1962
Afternoon
Liverpool, Cavern Club.
Evening
Chester, Riverpark Ballroom.
With Gerry & the Pacemakers.

31 August 1962
Lydney, Town Hall.

1 September 1962
Stroud, Subscription Rooms.

2 September 1962
Liverpool, Cavern Club.

3 September 1962
Afternoon
Liverpool, Cavern Club.
Evening
Widnes, Queen's Hall. With Billy Kramer & the Coasters, Rory Storm & the Hurricanes.

4 September 1962
London, EMI Studios, Abbey Road.
Recording of the Beatles debut single *Love Me Do*.

5 September 1962
Liverpool, Cavern Club.

6 September 1962
Afternoon
Liverpool, Cavern Club.
Evening
Liverpool, Rialto Ballroom.
The Beatles Show. With the Big Three, the Mersey Beats, Rory Storm & the Hurricanes.

7 September 1962
Irby, Village Hall, Newton Dancing School.

8 September 1962
Birkenhead, YMCA. Birkenhead, Majestic
Ballroom.

9 September 1962
Liverpool, Cavern Club.
With Billy Kramer & the Coasters, Clinton Ford.

10 September 1962
Afternoon
Liverpool, Cavern Club.
Evening
Widnes, Queen's Hall.
With Rory Storm & the Hurricanes,
Geoff Stacey & the Wanderers.

11 September 1962
London, EMI Studios, Abbey Road.
New recording of the debut single
Love Me Do with Andy White on drums.

12 September 1962
Liverpool, Cavern Club.
With Freddie & the Dreamers, and as
backing band for Simone Jackson.

13 September 1962
Afternoon
Liverpool, Cavern Club.
Evening
Chester, Riverpark Ballroom.

14 September 1962
New Brighton, Tower Ballroom.
Operation Big Beat 5, with the Beatles
and five bands.

15 September 1962
Northwich, Victory Memorial Hall.

16 September 1962
Liverpool, Cavern Club.

17 September 1962
Afternoon
Liverpool, Cavern Club.
Evening
Widnes, Queen's Hall.
With Billy Kramer & the Coasters, the Vikings.

The poster for the concerts
at Queen's Hall on 3, 10 and 17
September 1962.

19 and 20 September 1962
Liverpool, Cavern Club.

21 September 1962
New Brighton, Tower Ballroom.
With Rory Storm & the Hurricanes.

22 September 1962
Birkenhead, Majestic Ballroom.

23 September 1962
Liverpool, Cavern Club.
With the Saints Jazz Band, the Dominoes.

25 September 1962
Heswall, Barnston Women's Institute,
Heswall Jazz Club.

26 September 1962
Afternoon
Liverpool, Cavern Club.
Evening
Liverpool, Cavern Club.
With the Spidermen, the Dominoes.

28 September 1962
Afternoon
Liverpool, Cavern Club.
Evening
Mersey River, show onboard the "Royal Irish".
With Lee Castle & the Barons.

29 September 1962
Manchester, Oasis Club.

30 September 1962
Liverpool, Cavern Club.
With the Red River Jazzmen,
Clay Ellis & the Raiders.

2 October 1962
Liverpool, Cavern Club.

3 October 1962
Liverpool, Cavern Club.
With the Echoes, Billy Kramer & the Coasters.

4 October 1962
Liverpool, Cavern Club.

6 October 1962
Birkenhead-Port Sunlight, Hulme Hall.

7 October 1962
Liverpool, Cavern Club.
With the Red River Jazzmen,
the Bluegenes, the Zodiacs.

8 October 1962
EMI House, Manchester Square, London.
Recording for the show "Friday Spectacular" on
Radio Luxembourg, broadcast on 12 October.
The Beatles played before an audience using
playback and performed *Love Me Do*
and *P.S. I Love You.*

10 October 1962
Afternoon
Liverpool, Cavern Club.
Evening
Liverpool, Cavern Club.
With the Four Jays, Ken Dallas
& the Silhouettes.

11 October 1962
Liverpool, Rialto Ballroom.

12 October 1962
Afternoon
Liverpool, Cavern Club.
Evening
New Brighton, Tower Ballroom.
"Little Richard at the Tower".
With Little Richard, the Big Three, the Dakotas,
Pete MacLaine, Billy Kramer & the Coasters, the
Undertakers, Rory Storm & the Hurricanes, Lee
Curtis & the All Stars, the Mersey Beats,
Gus Tryvis & the Midnighters,
Peppermint Twisters, Four Jays.
Radio Luxembourg broadcast of *Love Me Do*
and *P.S. I Love You.*

A letter signed by John Lennon dated 22 October 1962. He requests the National Health Service to reinstate his name on their lists explaining that he had left the country only for an engagement as a musician in Germany. At the bottom of the letter, the health service bureau has noted that he was reinserted on 25/10/1962.

251, Menlove Avenue, Liverpool 18.

22nd October 1962

REF: R.28/LIP

The National Health Service,
Liverpool Executive Council,
36, Princes Road,
LIVERPOOL 8.

Dear Sir,

I have received your letter of the 1st instant to say that you have been informed that I left this country in July 1960. In point of fact I left the country only for an engagement (as a musician) in Germany but returned to this country about three months later. I would, therefore be obliged if you would please return my name to the National Health Service List.

Yours faithfully,
John Lennon.

13 October 1962
Liverpool, Cavern Club.
With the Zenith Six, Group One.

15 October 1962
Birkenhead, Majestic Ballroom.

16 October 1962
Runcorn, La Scala Ballroom.

17 October 1962
Afternoon
Liverpool, Cavern Club.
Granada TV, Manchester.
For the programme "People and Places".
The Beatles performed:
Kansas City / Hey-Hey-Hey-Hey!
Some Other Guy
Love Me Do.

Evening
Liverpool, Cavern Club.
With the Big Three, Group One.

19 October 1962
Liverpool, Cavern Club.

20 October 1962
Hull, Majestic Ballroom.

21 October 1962
Liverpool, Cavern Club.

22 October 1962
Widnes, Queen's Hall.
With the Mersey Beats,
Lee Curtis & the All Stars.

25 October 1962
Playhouse Theatre, St. John's Rd., Manchester.
Recording for the 26 October episode
of the programme "Here We Go".
The Beatles recorded:
Sheila
Love Me Do
A Taste of Honey
P.S. I Love You.

26 October 1962
Afternoon
Liverpool, Cavern Club. BBC Radio,
"Here We Go".
Presenter: Ray Peters
Producer: Peter Pilbeam
Songs broadcast:
Love Me Do (2:20)
A Taste of Honey (2:15)
P.S. I Love You (2:00).
Evening
Preston, Public Hall.

27 October 1962
Birkenhead-Port Sunlight, Hulme Hall.

28 October 1962
Liverpool, Empire Theatre.
With Little Richard, Craig Douglas, Jet Harris
& the Jetblacks, Kenny Lynch, the Sounds
Incorporated, the Breakaways, and as backing
band for Craig Douglas.

29 October 1962
Liverpool, Cavern Club.
Live recording for the Granada TV programme
"People and Places" of 2 November 1962.
The Beatles performed *Love Me Do* and
A Taste of Honey.

The Beatles returned to Hamburg twice during the latter part of 1962. The first time was from 1-14 November, and the second, from 18-31 December.

During their first stay the Beatles played at the Star-Club with Little Richard, who was billed as the main artist. The band then returned home for a series of concerts and performances for BBC Radio. An important second visit to the Abbey Road EMI studios then followed when the Beatles recorded their second single.

The session took place on 26 November (the record would be released on 11 January 1963). The Beatles recorded *Please Please Me* and *Ask Me Why*, respectively side A and B of this second single. After this session, another series of concerts followed organised by Epstein. These shows further contributed to the popularity of the band in Britain. In fact, the shows were extended until 17 December. On 18 December, the Beatles returned for the fifth time to Hamburg where they performed from 18-31 December. They were back in Britain for the New Year 1963... and the glory that was awaiting them.

Here are the details of the appearances of the Beatles for the end of 1962:

1-14 November 1962
Hamburg, Star-Club.
With Little Richard, Johnny & the Hurricanes,
the Strangers, King Size Taylor, Tony Sheridan &
the Star-Combo, Carol Elvin.

11 November 1962
Broadcasting of part of the performance already
shown on 17 October 1962 by Granada TV.
During the programme "Know the North" the
song *Some Other Guy* was broadcast.

16 November 1962
EMI House, Manchester Square, London.
Recording for the Radio Luxembourg
programme "Friday Spectacular" that was
broadcast on 23 November. The Beatles
performed *Love Me Do* and *P.S. I Love You*.

17 November 1962
Coventry, Matrix Hall.

18 November 1962
Liverpool, Cavern Club.
With the Mersey Beats.

19 November 1962
Afternoon
Liverpool, Cavern Club.
Evening
West Bromwich, Adelphi Ballroom.
Cancellation of an engagement
planned at Smethwich.

20 November 1962
Southport, Floral Hall.

21 November 1962
Afternoon
Liverpool, Cavern Club.
Evening
Liverpool, Cavern Club.
With the Zodiacs, Johnny Templer & the Hi-Cats.

22 November 1962
Birkenhead, Majestic Ballroom.

23 November 1962
St. James Hall, Gloucester Terrace, London W2.
BBC audition for the TV show "Lunchtime
Audition". On 27 November the BBC advised the
Beatles that they had been deemed
suitable for the programme.
Broadcasting of the Radio Luxembourg
programme "Friday Spectacular",
recorded on 16 November.
New Brighton, Tower Ballroom.
With the Llew Hird Jazz Band, Billy Kramer
& the Coasters, the Clan McCleod Pipe Band.

24 November 1962
Prestatyn, Royal Lido Ballroom.

25 November 1962
Liverpool, Cavern Club.
With the Zenith Six, the Four Mosts,
the Dennisons.

26 November 1962
London, EMI Studios, Abbey Road.
Recording of the Beatles' second single
Please Please Me / Ask Me Why.

27 November 1962
The BBC Paris Theatre,
Lower Regent St., London SW1.
Rehearsal and recording of the show "Talent Spot"
that would be broadcast on 4 December 1962.
The Beatles performed:
Love Me Do
P.S. I Love You
Twist and Shout

28 November 1962
Afternoon
Liverpool, Cavern Club. With the Remo Four,
Dee Young & the Pontiacs.

Evening
Liverpool, Lewis's Department Store, 527 Club.

29 November 1962
Birkenhead, Majestic Ballroom.

30 November 1962
Afternoon
Liverpool, Cavern Club.
Evening
Earlestown, Town Hall.

1 December 1962
Evening
Northwich, Victory Memorial Hall.
From midnight
New Brighton, Tower Ballroom.

2 December 1962
Peterborough, Embassy Cinema.
With Frank Ifield, Ted Taylor,
Julie Grant, Susan Cope.
The Beatles performed:
A Taste of Honey, *Love Me Do*, *Twist and Shout*

3 December 1962
TWW TV Studios, Bristol.
Live broadcast performance for the programme
"Discs-A-GoGo". The Beatles performed *Love Me Do*.

4 December 1962
Kingsway Studio, London ATV Television.
Live broadcast performance for the programme
"Tuesday Rendez-Vous".
The Beatles performed *Love Me Do*.
Broadcasting of the programme "Talent Spot"
recorded on 27 November.
Presenter: Gary Marshal
Producer: Brian Willey
With the Ted Taylour Four, Mark Tracey,
Elkie Brooks, Frank Kelly.
The following were broadcast:
Love Me Do (2:20)

P.S. I Love You (2:00)
Twist and Shout (2:15)

5 December 1962
Liverpool, Cavern Club.

6 December 1962
Southport, Queen's Hotel,
Club Django.

7 December 1962
Afternoon
Liverpool, Cavern Club.
Evening
New Brighton, Tower Ballroom.

8 December 1962
Manchester, Oasis Club.

9 December 1962
Liverpool, Cavern Club.
George Martin and Judy Lockhart-Smith
attend the show.

10 December 1962
Liverpool, Cavern Club.

11 December 1962
Runcorn, La Scala Ballroom.
With Johnny Sandon, the Remo Four,
the Mersey Beats.

12 December 1962
Afternoon
Liverpool, Cavern Club.
Evening
Liverpool, Cavern Club. With Gerry &
the Pacemakers.

13 December 1962
Bedford, Corn Exchange.

14 December 1962
Shrewsbury, Music Hall.

15 December 1962
Afternoon
Birkenhead, Majestic Ballroom.
From midnight
Birkenhead, Majestic Ballroom.
"Mersey Beat" 1962 Poll Awards Show.
With Lee Curtis & the All Stars.

16 December 1962
Liverpool, Cavern Club.

17 December 1962
Granada TV Studio, Manchester.
Live broadcast performance for the
programme "People and Places".
The Beatles performed *Love Me Do*
and *A Taste of Honey*.

18-31 December 1962
(25 December day off)
Hamburg, Star-Club.
With Johnny & the Hurricanes, King Size Taylor
& the Dominoes, Carol Elvin, the Strangers,
Tony Sheridan & the Star-Combo.
The show on 31 December (performance
by the completely inebriated Beatles)
was tape recorded by King Size Taylor:
I'm Gonna Sit Right Down and Cry (Over You)
I Saw Her Standing There (with Horst Fascher)
Roll Over Beethoven
the Hippy Hippy Shake
Sweet Little Sixteen
Lend Me Your Comb
Your Feet's Too Big
Twist and Shout
Mr. Moonlight
A Taste of Honey
Besame Mucho
Reminiscing
Kansas City
Where Have You Been (All My Life)?
Till There Was You

Nothin' Shakin' (But the Leaves on the Trees)
To Know Her Is to Love Her
Little Queenie
Falling in Love Again
Ask Me Why
Be-Bop-A-Lula (voc. Manfred Fascher)
Hallelujah, I Love Her So (voc. Horst Fascher)
Sheila
Red Sails in the Sunset
Everybody's Trying to Be My Baby
Matchbox
I'm Talking About You
(I Do the) Shimmy Shimmy
Long Tall Sally
I Remember You
Red Hot
Love Me Do

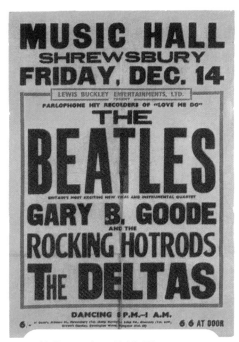

**14 December 1962. The poster
for the concert at Shrewsbury
Music Hall.**

1963

A whirlwind of concerts, radio and television

The year 1962 drew to a close and it was already 1963. After that, nothing would ever be the same... 1963 definitively crowned the success of the Beatles. It was the year their name went down in history. But let's not rush ahead just yet.

In January 1963 the band left on a short tour of five dates in Scotland, one of which was cancelled (on 2 January) because of a snowstorm that kept their plane from landing in Edinburg.

Scotland Tour

3 January 1963
Elgin, Two Red Shoes Ballroom.

4 January 1963
Dingwall, Town Hall.

5 January 1963
Bridge of Allan, Museum Hall. With Roy Purdon & the Telstars.

6 January 1963
Aberdeen, Beach Ballroom.

The Beatles wear the suits with collarless jackets designed for them by Pierre Cardin.

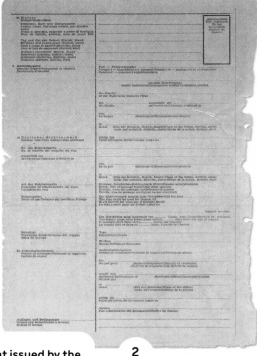

1 and 2. **Document issued by the German border police authorizing John Lennon to reside in Hamburg in January 1963.**

After the tour, the Beatles appeared on the children's programme "Round-Up" broadcast live from Glasgow. They used playback and performed *Please Please Me*, their single about to be released. The band then went back to Liverpool where they performed on 10 January. Their engagements continued, interspersed with occasional tours. First there was a tour as backing band for Helen Shapiro, and then with Tommy Roe & Chris Montez. In both cases, however, it only took a few days before the Beatles started taking centre stage, and became the true stars of the shows.

8 January 1963
Glasgow, Scottish TV.
Live performance for the programme "Round-Up". The Beatles performed *Please Please Me*.

10 January 1963
Liverpool, Cavern Club.

11 January 1963
Afternoon
Liverpool, Cavern Club.
Evening
Old Hill, Plaza Ballroom.

12 January 1963
Chatham, Invicta Ballroom.

13 January 1963
ABC TV Studios,
Aston Road North, Birmingham.
Recording of the episode "Thank Your
Lucky Stars" of 19 January.
The Beatles performed *Please Please Me*
and *Ask Me Why*.

14 January 1963
Ellesmere Port, Civic Hall.

16 January 1963
Granada TV Centre, Playhouse Theatre,
St. John's Rd., Manchester.
Live broadcast of "People and Places".
The Beatles performed *Please Please Me*
and *Ask Me Why*.
Recording of the radio show "Here We Go"
broadcast on 25 January.
The Beatles performed:
Chains
Please Please Me
Ask Me Why
Three Cool Cats.

17 January 1963
Afternoon
Liverpool, Cavern Club.
Evening
Birkenhead, Majestic Ballroom.

18 January 1963
Morecambe, Floral Hall Ballroom.

19 January 1963
Whitchurch, Town Hall Ballroom.

Broadcasting of the show "Thank Your Lucky
Stars" recorded on 13 January. The Beatles
performed *Please Please Me* and *Ask Me Why*.

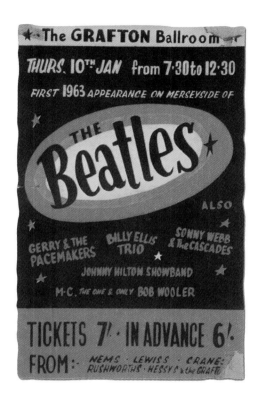

Above: **10 January 1963,
the poster of the concert at
Grafton Ballroom.**
Below: **The record *Please Please Me*.**

20 January 1963
Liverpool, Cavern Club.

21 January 1963
EMI House, Manchester Square, London.
Recording in front of a live audience of the
25 January show "Friday Spectacular".

22 January 1963
Afternoon
Playhouse Theatre,
Northumberland Ave., London WC2.
Recording for the 26 January
broadcast of "Saturday Club".
Evening
Paris Theatre,
Lower Regent St., London SW1.
Recording for the 29 January broadcast
of "the Talent Spot".

23 January 1963
Liverpool, Cavern Club.

24 January 1963
Mold, Assembly Hall.

25 January 1963
Darwen, Co-operative Hall.
With the Mustangs, Electones,
Mike Taylor Combo.

Broadcast of the Radio Luxembourg programme
"Friday Spectacular" recorded on 21 January.
The Beatles performed:
Lend Me Your Comb
Carol
Please Please Me
Ask Me Why.

Broadcasting of the programme "Here We Go"
recorded on 16 January.
Presenter: Ray Peters.
Producer: Peter Pilbeam.

The Beatles performed:
Chains
Please Please Me
Ask Me Why
Three Cool Cats (recorded but not broadcast).

26 January 1963
Broadcasting of the programme "Saturday Club"
recorded on 22 January.
Presenter: Brian Matthew
Producer: Jimmy Grant
The Beatles performed:
Some Other Guy
Love Me Do
Please Please Me
Keep Your Hands off My Baby
Beautiful Dreamer

Macclesfield, El Rio Club Dance Hall.
With Wayne Fontana & the Jets.

Stoke-on-Trent, King's Hall.

27 January 1963
Morning and Afternoon
Rehearsal at the Cavern for the tour with H. Shapiro.
Evening
Manchester, Three Coins Club.

28 January 1963
Newcastle-upon-Tyne, Majestic Ballroom.

29 January 1963
Broadcasting of the programme "the Talent
Spot" recorded on 22 January.
Presenter: Gary Marshal
Producer: Brian Willey
The Beatles performed:
Please Please Me
Ask Me Why
Some Other Guy

30 January 1963
Liverpool, Cavern Club.

31 January 1963
Afternoon
Liverpool, Cavern Club.
Evening
Birkenhead, Majestic Ballroom.
With Freddie Starr &
the Midnighters, Johnny Quickly
& the Challengers.

1 February 1963
Tamworth, Assembly Rooms.
Sutton Coldfield, Maney Hall.

2 February 1963
Broadcasting of the programme
"Thank Your Lucky Stars".
The Beatles performed *Twist and Shout*
using playback.

Helen Shapiro Tour
With Helen Shapiro, Sanny Williams, Kenny
Lynch, the Kestrels, the Red Price Orchestra,
the Honeys, Dave Allen. The Beatles
occasionally performed *Love Me Do* and
Beautiful Dreamer during the tour.

2 February 1963
Launch of the tour that was
to begin on 5 February.
Bradford, Gaumont Cinema
(show recorded by ATV).
The Beatles performed:
Chains
Keep Your Hands off My Baby
A Taste of Honey
Please Please Me.

3 February 1963
Liverpool, Cavern Club. R&B Marathon.

4 February 1963
Liverpool, Cavern Club.

First Part of Helen Shapiro Tour

5 February 1963
Doncaster, Gaumont Cinema.

6 February 1963
Bedford, Granada Cinema.

7 February 1963
Wakefield, Regal Cinema.

8 February 1963
Carlisle, ABC Cinema.

9 February 1963
Sunderland, Empire Theatre.

End of First Part of Helen Shapiro Tour

11 February 1963
EMI Studios, London.
Recording of ten songs for the album
Please Please Me. the above was a day that
became legendary... How to record almost an
entire album in 585 minutes effectively in the
studio and ... live happily... someone would say
afterwards. The Beatles recorded ten songs.
The two singles that had already been released
were added to these songs to make up the
band's first LP.

12 February 1963
Sheffield-Gleadless, Arena Ballroom.
With Mark Stone & the Aidens, Screaming Lord
Sutch & the Savages, Frank Kelly & the Hunters,
Ian Crawford & the Boomerangs, the Brook
Brothers, the R&B Plus One Group, Freddie & the
Dreamers, Shane Fenton & the Fentones.

Oldham, Astoria Ballroom.

The posters for the concerts at the Azena Ballroom (12 February 1963) and at City Hall (2 March 1963) as backing band for Helen Shapiro. The first of the two announces that the Beatles are number one on the singles charts with *Please Please Me*.

13 February 1963
Hull, Majestic Ballroom.

14 February 1963
Liverpool, Locarno Ballroom.

15 February 1963
Birmingham-King's Heath, Ritz Ballroom.

16 February 1963
Oxford, Carfax Assembly Rooms.

17 February 1963
Cavern Club, Liverpool.

Recording for the programme "Thank Your Lucky Stars" broadcast on 23 February.

18 February 1963
Widnes, Queen's Hall.
With Buddy Britten & the Regents,
the Mersey Beats.

19 February 1963
Liverpool, Cavern Club.
With Lee Curtis & the All-Stars.

20 February 1963
Doncaster, Swimming Baths.

This photo, just as others in this chapter taken by photographer Dezo Hoffman, were massively used by British magazines to promote the image of the band in the country.

Playhouse Theatre,
Northumberland Ave., London.
Live broadcast performance for the BBC Radio
programme "Parade of the Pops".
Presenter: Denny Piercy
Producer: John Kingdon
The Beatles performed *Love Me Do* and
Please Please Me.

21 February 1963
Birkenhead, Majestic Ballroom.

22 February 1963
Manchester, Oasis Club.

23 February 1963
Broadcasting of the programme "Thank Your
Lucky Stars" recorded on 17 February.
the Beatles performed *Please Please Me*
using playback.

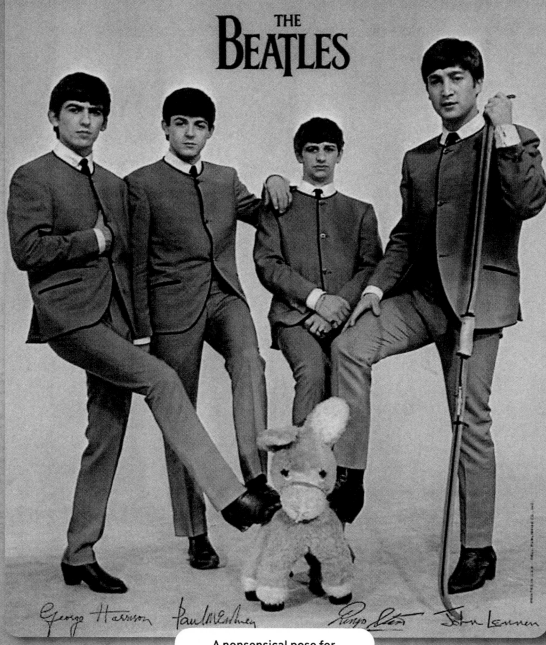

© NEMS ENT. LTD.

THE BEATLES

George Harrison   Paul McCartney   Ringo Starr   John Lennon

A nonsensical pose for
a publicity photo
of the Beatles taken early
in their career.

Second Part of Helen Shapiro Tour

23 February 1963
Mansfield, Granada Cinema.

24 February 1963
Coventry, Coventry Theatre.

Helen Shapiro Tour interrupted

25 February 1963
Leigh, Casino Ballroom.

Helen Shapiro Tour resumed

26 February 1963
Taunton, Gaumont Cinema
(Helen Shapiro was ill and was
replaced by Billie Davis).

27 February 1963
York, Rialto Theatre
(Helen Shapiro was ill and was
replaced by Billie Davis).

28 February 1963
Shrewsbury, Granada Cinema.

1 March 1963
Southport, Odeon Cinema.

2 March 1963
Sheffield, City Hall.

3 March 1963
Hanley, Gaumont Cinema.

End of Helen Shapiro Tour.

4 March 1963
St. Helens, Plaza Ballroom.

5 March 1963
EMI Studios, London.
The Beatles recorded:
From Me to You
Thank You Girl
The One After 99

6 March 1963
Playhouse Theatre, St. John's Rd., Manchester.
Recording of the programme "Here We Go"
broadcast on 12 March.

7 March 1963
Nottingham, Elizabethan Ballroom.
With Gerry & the Pacemakers, the Big Three,
Billy J. Kramer & the Dakotas.

8 March 1963
Harrogate, the Royal Hall.

Tour with Tommy Roe and Chris Montez
The Beatles were on the bill with the Viscounts,
Debbie Lee, Tony Marsh, and
Terry Young Six/Five.
The Beatles' programme consisted of the songs:
Love Me Do
Misery
A Taste of Honey
Do You Want to Know a Secret?
Please Please Me
I Saw Her Standing There.

9 March 1963
London-East Ham, Granada Cinema.

10 March 1963
Birmingham, Hippodrome Theatre.

Tommy Roe and Chris Montez Tour
Interrupted

11 March 1963
EMI House, Manchester Square, London.
Recording of the Radio Luxembourg
programme "Friday Spectacular"
broadcast on 15 March.

12 March 1963
Broadcasting of the programme "Here We Go"
recorded on 6 March. Presenter: Ray Peters.
Producer: Peter Pilbeam. With the Trad Lads,
Ben Richmond, the Northern Dance Orchestra.
The Beatles performed:
Misery
Do You Want to Know a Secret?
Please Please Me
I Saw Her Standing There (recorded but
not broadcast)

Tommy Roe and Chris Montez Tour resumed

12 March 1963
Bedford, Granada Cinema
(only three of the Beatles
performed as John was ill).
The show was recorded by BBC Radio.

13 March 1963
York, Rialto Theatre
(Only three of the Beatles
performed as John was ill).
Before the show, the three went to the EMI
studios to record the harmonica overdubbings
for *Thank You Girl.*

14 March 1963
Wolverhampton, Gaumont Cinema
(Only three of the Beatles
performed as John was ill).

15 March 1963
Bristol, Colston Hall.
Broadcasting of the Radio Luxembourg
programme "Friday Spectacular"
recorded on 11 March.
The Beatles performed *Please Please Me*
and *Ask Me Why.*

16 March 1963
Sheffield, City Hall.
Live broadcast performance for the programme
"Saturday Club". Studio 3A, Broadcasting House,
Portland Place, London W1.
Presenter: Brian Matthew
Producer: Jimmy Grant & Bernie Andrews
The Beatles performed:
I Saw Her Standing There
Misery
Too Much Monkey Business
I'm Talking About You
Please Please Me
the Hippy Hippy Shake.

17 March 1963
Peterborough, Embassy Cinema.

18 March 1963
Gloucester, Regal Cinema.

19 March 1963
Cambridge, Regal Cinema.

20 March 1963
Romford, ABC Cinema.

21 March 1963
Studio 1, Piccadilly Theatre,
Denmark St., London W1.
Recording for the programme "On the Scene"
broadcast on 28 March 1963.

Croydon-West, ABC Cinema.

The record She Loves You.

22 March 1963
Doncaster, Gaumont Cinema.

23 March 1963
Newcastle-Upon-Tyne, City Hall.

24 March 1963
Liverpool, Empire Theatre.

26 March 1963
Mansfield, Granada Cinema.

27 March 1963
Northampton, ABC Cinema.

28 March 1963
Exeter, ABC Cinema. Broadcasting
of the programme "On the Scene"
recorded on 21 March.
Presenter: Craig Douglas.
Producer: Brian Willey.
The Beatles performed:
Misery
Do You Want to Know a Secret?
Please Please Me.

29 March 1963
London-Lewisham, Odeon Cinema.

30 March 1963
Portsmouth, Guildhall.

31 March 1963
Leicester, De Montfort Hall.

**End of Tommy Roe and
Chris Montez Tour**

The first three months of 1963 were a daunting exploit for the Beatles that consisted of two tours, the recording of a complete LP, and dozens of appearances on radio and television. The Beatles were definitely making a living now!

On 12 April the Beatles' third single *From Me to You* was released. By 27 April it was topping the charts. In the meantime, John and Cynthia had the time to become parents to a baby boy named Julian. In May, John left for Spain with Brian. The trip, universally referred to as their "Spanish honeymoon", fuelled quite a lot of gossip about the sexual preferences of both.

On 18 April the Beatles went on tour with Roy Orbison, who was already a big star. Nevertheless, very soon he met the same fate as his predecessors, that is, he was obliged to concede the top billing to the Beatles... by popular acclaim.

Paul celebrated his twenty-first birthday on 18 June at his aunt's house, since the family's home was besieged by a hysterical mob of fans. In Liverpool, the girls started to practice a rather strange sport. They would stand in line at certain bus stops hoping to get on the bus that George Harrison's father was driving.

In July the first issue of the monthly the Beatles Book appeared. The magazine was published in association with the Official Beatles Fan Club and was entirely devoted to the band. The fan club of the Beatles had become, thanks to the popularity of the Fab Four, almost a paramilitary organisation. In the beginning, relations with the fans were managed by just one person, Miss Freda Kelly. She had her headquarters in the NEMS Liverpool offices. With the exponential increase in her workload, however, one of Brian's employees, Tony Barrow, came onboard to reorganise it all. He first divided the Club into two sections: one for the north of England, headed by Freda Kelly in Liverpool, and the other for the south, under the responsibility of a young woman named Bettina Rose. Over the years Bettina's offices on Monmouth Street in London became legendary.

Then, in a stroke of genius, Barrow created (literally) a third person, a "national secretary", that is, Anne Collingham. Though this person did not exist, her signature appeared on every newsletter put out by the Official Beatles Fan Club.

Now the creation of Anne Collingham might seem a minor detail, but quite the contrary. In fact it was NEMS itself that managed everything and over the years, when permission was sought for the opening of Fan Club branches abroad, it was Collingham, or rather the NEMS, and therefore the Beatles themselves, who issued official authorisation. In Italy, for example, the authorisation was issued to Miss Roxana Lanfiuti Baldi, historic president of the Italian fan club located in Cagliari. The Italian fan club eventually counted as many as fifteen regional offices that managed local events and issues. A mammoth organisation.

And also extremely rigid, as shown for example by correspondence of infinite historical value (for it indisputably clarifies the way the Beatles saw things). This was a letter sent on 31 December 1965 to Miss R. Cavicchioli in Rome in response to her request for official recognition of her fans organisation. Michael Crowther-Smith, office manager of the English Official Beatles Fan Club, replied in his letter that though the fan club would be happy to have a headquarters in Italy's capital, the only Club to have received official recognition was the one headed by Miss Baldi. The only way therefore to be officially recognized by the Beatles as a fan club, was to be recognized by Miss Baldi. Any other initiative, the letter clearly

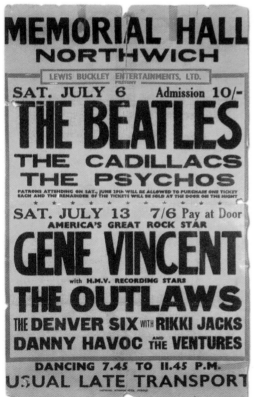

14 June 1963 poster: The Beatles and Gerry & the Pacemakers at the New Brighton Tower; 22 June 1963 (Town Hall Ballroom): The Beatles are by now the top attraction on the bill; 6 July 1963 (Memorial Hall, Northwich): The Beatles top the bill even surpassing their old idol Gene Vincent.

stated, would be an infringement of the Beatles' copyright. This was not only true in theory, but also in practice. And in fact this system is still in force today. The president of the Official Beatles Fan Club — who after some years added "Pepperland" to the denomination — is still Miss Roxana Lanfiuti Baldi. All of the other organisations are guilty of an infringement of the copyright of the Beatles' name and are not officially recognized...

After this rather long digression on the history of The Beatles fan clubs, let us return to our Fab Four. They are now busy recording their fourth single, *She Loves You*. In the meantime in Britain, not only was Beatlemania gathering momentum, but so was the Profumo affair. And this might have been what gave the band... their final boost to stardom, at least in Britain. Indeed the powerful Fleet Street lobby of journalists, to distract the public's attention from the embarrassing details of the Profumo case, turned attention to the (yet to be generally recognized) collective craze for the four boys from Liverpool.

In those days the subjects of Her Majesty the Queen were surely wondering whether their ailing empire would collapse first from the shockwaves caused by the Beatles, or from the sexual antics of their Secretary of State for War, John Profumo. The Fab Four from Liverpool, in the meantime, continued their skyrocket to glory.

1 April 1963
Studio 1, Piccadilly Theatre,
Denmark St., London W1.
Recording for two BBC radio broadcasts of the programme "Side by Side", broadcast on 22 April and 13 May.

3 April 1963
Playhouse Theatre,
Northumberland Ave., London WC2.
Recording for the programme "Easy Beat" broadcast on 7 April.

4 April 1963
BBC Paris Theatre,
Lower Regent St., London SW1.
Recording for the programme "Side by Side" broadcast on 24 June.

Stowe, Stowe School, Roxburgh Hall.

5 April 1963
London, EMI House.
An in-house show for the EMI employees. This was also the occasion for the presentation of the Silver Single for sales of Please Please Me. It was the first of an impressive series of Beatles' hits that eventually set a Guinness record. That evening the Beatles played at the Swimming Bath of Leyton.

6 April 1963
Buxton, Pavilion Gardens Ballroom.
With the Trixons.

7 April 1963
Broadcasting of the programme "Easy Beat" recorded on 3 April.
Presenter: Brian Matthew.
Producer: Ron Belchier.

The Beatles performed
Please Please Me and *Misery*.
Presentation by Gerry Marsden
of *From Me to You*.

Portsmouth-Southsea, Savoy Ballroom.

9 April 1963
London-Kilburn,
Gaumont State Cinema Ballroom.
With Gerry & the Pacemakers.
The Beatles performed:
Love Me Do
Please Please Me
Twist and Shout
A Taste of Honey
Baby It's You
From Me to You.

Kingsway Studios, London. Live performance on
the show "Tuesday Rendez-Vous".

10 April 1963
Birkenhead, Majestic Ballroom.
Show recorded by BBC TV.

11 April 1963
Middleton, Cooperative Hall.
With Shaun & Sum People.

12 April 1963
Liverpool, Cavern Club
R&B Marathon No. 2. With the Dennisons,
Faron's Flamingoes, the Roadrunners.

13 April 1963
Lime Grove Studios, London.
Recording for the programme "6:25 Show"
broadcast on 16 April.
the Beatles performed:
From Me to You, Thank You Girl,
Please Please Me.
They were accompanied by the BBC Orchestra.

14 April 1963
ABC TV Studios, Teddington, London.
Recording for the programme "Thank Your
Lucky Stars" broadcast on 20 April.
the Beatles performed *From Me to You*.

15 April 1963
Tenbury Wells, Bridge Hotel,
Riverside Dancing Club.

16 April 1963
Broadcasting of the programme "6:25 Show"
recorded on 13 April. The Beatles performed:
From Me to You, Thank You Girl,
Please Please Me.
They were accompanied by the BBC Orchestra.

Granada TV Studios, Manchester.
Live performance for the programme
"Scene at 6:30".

17 April 1963
Luton, Majestic Ballroom.

18 April 1963
Royal Albert Hall, Kensington Gore, London SW7.
Live performance for the BBC Radio programme
"Swingin' Sound '63".
Presenters: George Melly & Rolf Harris.
Producers: Terry Henebery & Ron Belchier.
The Beatles participated with 15
other bands and performed:
Please Please Me (not broadcast)
Misery (not broadcast)
Twist and Shout
From Me to You
Mack the Knife (together with the other bands).

19 April 1963
Stoke-on-Trent, King's Hall.
Mersey Beat Showcase 2.

With Gerry & the Pacemakers, the Big Three,
Billy J. Kramer & the Dakotas.
The Beatles performed *Please Please Me*.

20 April 1963
Frodsham, Mersey View
Pleasure Grounds Ballroom.
Broadcasting of the programme "Thank Your
Lucky Stars" recorded on 14 April.
The Beatles performed *From Me to You*.

21 April 1963
London, Wembley, Empire Pool & Sports Arena.
NME 1962-63 Annual Poll-winners' All-Star
Concert. With Cliff Richard & the Shadows,
and 14 other bands.
Recorded by ABC TV and broadcast on 28 April.
The Beatles performed:
Please Please Me
From Me to You
Twist and Shout
Long Tall Sally.

In the evening, the Beatles played at the
Pigalle Club of London.

22 April 1963
Broadcasting of the programme "Side by Side"
recorded on 1 April.
Presenter: John Dunn.
Producer: Bryant Marriott.
The Beatles performed:
Side by Side (with the Karl Denver Trio)
I Saw Her Standing There
Do You Want to Know a Secret?
Baby It's You
Please Please Me
From Me to You
Misery.

23 April 1963
Southport, Floral Hall.

24 April 1963
London, Finsbury Park, Majestic Ballroom.
Mersey Beat Showcase 3.
With Gerry & the Pacemakers, the Big Three,
Billy J. Kramer & the Dakotas.

25 April 1963
Croydon, Fairfield Hall Ballroom.
Mersey Beat Showcase 4. With Gerry & the
Pacemakers, the Big Three, Billy J. Kramer
& the Dakotas.

26 April 1963
Shrewsbury, Music Hall.

27 April 1963
Northwich, Victory Memorial Hall.

28 April 1963
Broadcasting of the NME 1962-63 Annual Poll-
Winners' All-Star Concert recorded on 21 April.
The Beatles performed:
Please Please Me
From Me to You
Twist and Shout
Long Tall Sally.

The Beatles went on holiday: John and Brian
to Spain; Paul, Ringo and George to Tenerife.

11 May 1963
Nelson, Imperial Ballroom.

12 May 1963
London, ABC TV Studios.
Recording for the programme "Thank Your
Lucky Stars" broadcast on 18 May.

13 May 1963
Broadcasting of the programme
"Side by Side" recorded on 1 April.
Presenter: John Dunn.
Producer: Bryant Marriott.
The Beatles performed:
Side by Side (with the Karl Denver Trio)
From Me to You
Long Tall Sally
A Taste of Honey
Chains
Thank You Girl
Boys.

14 May 1963
Sunderland, Rink Ballroom.

15 May 1963
Chester, Royalty Theatre.
Show recorded for the Granada TV
programme "Beat City".
The Beatles performed:
Some Other Guy
Thank You Girl
Do You Want to Know a Secret?
Please Please Me
You've Really Got a Hold on Me
I Saw Her Standing There
From Me to You.

16 May 1963
London, Shepherd's Bush Green.
Live broadcast of the programme
"Pops and Lenny".
The Beatles performed *From Me to You* and
Please Please Me, After You've Gone
(with the cast of the show).

17 May 1963
Norwich, Grosvenor Rooms.

18 May 1963
Broadcasting of the programme "Thank Your
Lucky Stars", recorded on 12 May.
The Beatles performed From Me to You and
I Saw Her Standing There.

Roy Orbison Tour Begins
Two concerts a day.
The Beatles shared the bill with Gerry & the
Pacemakers, David Macbeth, Louise Cordet,
Erky Grant & the Tonettes, Ian Crawford,
the Terry Young Six.
The Beatles performed:
Some Other Guy
Do You Want to Know a Secret?
Love Me Do
From Me to You
Please Please Me
I Saw Her Standing There
Twist and Shout.

18 May 1963
Slough, Adelphi Cinema.

19 May 1963
Hanley, Gaumont Cinema.

20 May 1963
Southampton, Gaumont Cinema.

21 May 1963
Playhouse Theatre, Northumberland Ave.,
London WC2.
Recording for the programme
"Saturday Club" broadcast on 25 May.
Recording for the programme "Steppin' Out"
broadcast on 3 June.

22 May 1963
Ipswich, Gaumont Cinema.

23 May 1963
Nottingham, Odeon Cinema.

24 May 1963
London-Walthamstow, Granada Cinema.
Studio 2, BBC Aeolian Hall,
135-137 New Bond St., London.
Recording for the programme "Pop Go the
Beatles" broadcast on 4 June.

25 May 1963
Broadcasting of the programme "Saturday Club",
recorded on 21 May.
Presenter: Brian Matthew.
Producers: Jimmy Grant & Bernie Andrews.
The Beatles performed:
I Saw Her Standing There
Do You Want to Know a Secret?
Boys
Long Tall Sally

From Me to You
Money (That's What I Want)

Sheffield, City Hall.
The Beatles were recorded live
for the BBC and performed:
Happy Birthday
Johnny B. Goode
Memphis Tennessee
You've Really Got a Hold on Me.

26 May 1963
Liverpool, Empire Theatre.

27 May 1963
Cardiff, Capitol Cinema.

28 May 1963
Worcester, Gaumont Cinema.

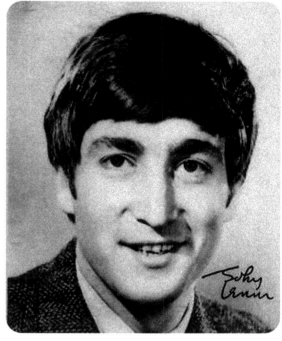

29 May 1963
York, Rialto Theatre.

30 May 1963
Manchester, Odeon Cinema.

31 May 1963
Southend-on-Sea, Odeon Cinema.

1 June 1963
London-Tooting, Granada Cinema.

BBC Paris Theatre,
Lower Regent St., London SW1.
Recording of the programme "Pop Go the
Beatles" broadcast on 18 June.
Recording of the programme "Pop Go the
Beatles" broadcast on 11 June.

2 June 1963
Brighton, Hippodrome Theatre.

3 June 1963
Broadcasting of the programme "Steppin' Out"
recorded on 21 May.
Presenter: Diz Disley
Producer: Terry Henebery
The Beatles performed:
Please Please Me
I Saw Her Standing There
Roll Over Beethoven
Thank You Girl
From Me to You
Twist and Shout (not broadcast).

London-Woolwich, Granada Cinema.

4 June 1963
Broadcasting of the programme "Pop Go the
Beatles" recorded on 24 May.
Presenter: Lee Peters.
Producer: Terry Henebery.
With the Lorne Gibson Trio.
The Beatles performed:
Pop Go the Beatles (theme song)
From Me to You
Everybody's Trying to Be My Baby
Do You Want to Know a Secret?
You've Really Got a Hold on Me
Misery
The Hippy Hippy Shake
Pop Go the Beatles (show theme song).

Birmingham, Town Hall.

5 June 1963
Leeds, Odeon Cinema.

7 June 1963
Glasgow, Odeon Cinema.

8 June 1963
Newcastle-Upon-Tyne, City Hall.

9 June 1963
Blackburn, King George's Hall.

End of the Roy Orbison Tour

10 June 1963
Bath, Pavilion.

11 June 1963
Broadcasting of the programme "Pop Go the
Beatles", recorded on 1 June.
Presenter: Lee Peters
Producer: Terry Henebery
With the Countrymen.
The Beatles performed:
Pop Go the Beatles (show theme song)

Too Much Monkey Business
I Got to Find My Baby
Young Blood
Baby It's You
Till There Was You
Love Me Do
Pop Go the Beatles (show theme song)

12 June 1963
Liverpool, Grafton Rooms
NSPCC Charity Concert.

13 June 1963
Stockport, Palace Theatre Club.
Manchester, Southern Sporting Club.

14 June 1963
New Brighton, Tower Ballroom.
Mersey Beat Showcase 5.
With Gerry & the Pacemakers and
six other bands.

15 June 1963
Salisbury, City Hall.

16 June 1963
Romford, Odeon Cinema.
Mersey Beat Showcase 6. With Gerry & the
Pacemakers, Billy J. Kramer & the Dakotas.

17 June 1963
Studio 5, BBC Maida Vale,
Delaware Rd., London W9.
Recording of the programme "Pop Go the
Beatles" broadcast on 25 June.

18 June 1963
Broadcasting of the programme "Pop Go the
Beatles" recorded on 1 June.
Presenter: Lee Peters.
Producer: Terry Henebery.
With Carter-Lewis & the Southerners.

The Beatles performed:
Pop Go the Beatles (show theme song)
A Shot of Rhythm and Blues
Memphis Tennessee
Happy Birthday to You (Paul)
A Taste of Honey
Sure to Fall (in Love with You)
Money (That's What I Want)
From Me to You
Pop Go the Beatles (show theme song)

19 June 1963
Playhouse Theatre,
Northumberland Ave., London WC2.
Recording of the programme "Easy Beat"
broadcast on 23 June.

21 June 1963
Guildford, Odeon Cinema.

22 June 1963
Abergavenny, Town Hall Ballroom.
(In the afternoon, John recorded an episode of
"Juke Box Jury" for the BBC. After the recording
session, a helicopter took him from London to
the Beatles' concert venue).

23 June 1963
Broadcasting of the programme "Easy Beat"
recorded on 19 June.
Presenter: Brian Matthew
Producer: Ron Belchier
The Beatles performed:
Some Other Guy
A Taste of Honey
Thank You Girl
From Me to You.

ALPHA TV Studios, Birmingham.
Recording for the programme "Lucky Stars
(Summer Spin)" broadcast on 29 June.

24 June 1963
Broadcasting of the programme
"Side by Side" recorded on 4 April.
Presenter: John Dunn
Producer: Bryant Marriott
The Beatles performed:
Side by Side (with the Karl Denver Trio,
recording of 1 April 1963)
Too Much Monkey Business
Love Me Do
Boys
I'll Be on My Way
From Me to You.

Playhouse Theatre,
Northumberland Ave., London WC2.
Recording of the programme "Saturday Club"
broadcast on 29 June.

25 June 1963
Broadcasting of the programme "Pop Go the
Beatles" recorded on 17 June.
Presenter: Lee Peters.
Producer: Terry Henebery.
With the Bachelors.
The Beatles performed:
Pop Go the Beatles (show theme song)
I Saw Her Standing There
Anna (Go to Him)
Boys
Chains
P.S. I Love You
Twist and Shout
Pop Go the Beatles (theme song)
A Taste of Honey (recorded but not broadcast)

Middlesbrough, Astoria Ballroom.

26 June 1963
Newcastle-upon-Tyne, Majestic Ballroom.

28 June 1963
Leeds, Queen's Hall.
With Mr. Acker Bilk's Paramount Jazz Band.

29 June 1963
Broadcasting of the programme "Saturday Club",
recorded on 24 June.
Presenter: Brian Matthew
Producers: Jimmy Grant & Bernie Andrews
The Beatles performed:
I Got to Find My Baby
Memphis Tennessee
Money (That's What I Want)
Till There Was You
From Me to You
Roll over Beethoven.

Broadcasting of the programme "Lucky Stars
(Summer Spin)", recorded on 23 June.
The Beatles performed *From Me to You* and
I Saw Her Standing There.

30 June 1963
Great Yarmouth, ABC Cinema.
Show recorded by the BBC.
The Beatles performed:
Some Other Guy
Thank You Girl
Do You Want to Know a Secret?
Misery
A Taste of Honey
I Saw Her Standing There
Love Me Do
From Me to You
Baby It's You
Please Please Me
Twist and Shout.

1 July 1963
EMI Studios, London.
Recording of the single *She Loves You /
I'll Get You.*

2 July 1963
Studio 5, BBC Maida Vale, Delaware Rd., London.
Recording of the programme "Pop Go the
Beatles" broadcast on 16 July.

3 July 1963
Playhouse Theatre, St. John's Rd., Manchester.
Recording of the programme "The Beat Show"
broadcast on 4 July.

4 July 1963
BBC Radio "The Beat Show", recorded on 3 July.
Presenter: Gay Byrne.
Producer: Geoff Lawrence.
The Beatles performed:
From Me to You
A Taste of Honey
Twist and Shout.

5 July 1963
Old Hill, Plaza Ballroom.
With Denny & the Diplomats.

6 July 1963
Northwich, Victory Memorial Hall.

7 July 1963
Blackpool, ABC Theatre.

8-13 July 1963
Margate, Winter Gardens.
With Billy J. Kramer & the Dakotas.
The Beatles performed:
Roll over Beethoven
Thank You Girl
Chains
Please Please Me
A Taste of Honey
I Saw Her Standing There
Baby It's You
From Me to You
Twist and Shout.

10 July 1963
Studio 2, BBC Aeolian Hall,
135-137 New Bond St., London.
Recording of the programme "Pop Go the
Beatles" broadcast on 22 July.
Recording of the programme "Pop Go the
Beatles" broadcast on 30 July.

14 July 1963
Blackpool, ABC Theatre.

16 July 1963
BBC Paris Theatre,
Lower Regent St., London SW1.
Recording of the programme "Pop Go the
Beatles" broadcast on 6 August.
Recording of the programme "Pop Go the
Beatles" broadcast on 13 August.
Recording of the programme "Pop Go the
Beatles" broadcast on 20 August.

Broadcasting of the programme "Pop Go the
Beatles" recorded on 2 July 1963.
Presenter: Rodney Burke
Producer: Terry Henebery
With Duffy Power & the Graham Bond Quartet
The Beatles performed:
Three Cool Cats (not broadcast)
Sweet Little Sixteen (not broadcast)
Ask Me Why (not broadcast)
Pop Go the Beatles (show theme song)
That's All Right (Mama)
There's a Place
Carol
Soldier of Love (Lay Down Your Arms)
Lend Me Your Comb
Clarabella
Pop Go the Beatles (show theme song)

17 July 1963
Playhouse Theatre,
Northumberland Ave., London WC2.
Recording for the programme "Easy Beat"
broadcast on 21 July.

18 July 1963
EMI Studios, London
Recording session for "With the Beatles".

19 and 20 July 1963
Rhyl, Ritz Ballroom.

21 July 1963
Blackpool, Queen's Theatre.

Broadcasting of the programme
"Easy Beat" recorded on 17 July.
Presenter: Brian Matthew
Producer: Ron Belchier
The Beatles performed
I Saw Her Standing There
A Shot of Rhythm and Blues
There's a Place
Twist and Shout.

22-27 July 1963
Weston-super-Mare, Odeon Cinema.
Two shows a day.
With Gerry & the Pacemakers, Tommy Quickly.

23 July 1963
Broadcasting of the programme
"Pop Go the Beatles" recorded on 10 July.
Presenter: Rodney Burke
Producer: Terry Henebery
With Carter-Lewis & the Southerners.
The Beatles performed:
Pop Go the Beatles (show theme song)
Sweet Little Sixteen
A Taste of Honey

Nothin' Shakin' (But the Leaves on the Tree)
Love Me Do
Lonesome Tears in My Eyes
So How Come (No One Loves Me)
Pop Go the Beatles (show theme song).

28 July 1963
Great Yarmouth, ABC Cinema.

30 July 1963
Broadcasting of the programme "Pop Go the Beatles"
recorded on 10 July.
Presenter: Rodney Burke
Producer: Terry Henebery
With the Searchers.
The Beatles performed:
Pop Go the Beatles (show theme song)
Memphis Tennessee
Do You Want to Know a Secret?
Till There Was You

Matchbox
Please Mr. Postman
the Hippy Hippy Shake
Pop Go the Beatles (show theme song).

EMI Studios, London.
Recording session for "With the Beatles".

Playhouse Theatre,
Northumberland Ave., London WC2.
Recording of the programme "Saturday Club"
broadcast on 24 August.

31 July 1963
Nelson, Imperial Ballroom.

The path to myth

As we were saying, that summer of '63 was problematic for the United Kingdom. Repercussions continued from the Profumo affair. In addition, during that time a group of merry thieves pulled off a colossal robbery of a Royal Mail train. The result became known as the Great Train Robbery and yielded over £2.6 million in loot! Perhaps this was the reason why the press, united as never before since the bombing of London, decided to create an issue that would distract the public from the incredible series of "misfortunes" to which the country had fallen?

In any case, in October, newspapers suddenly headlined "Disorder!" with full pages relating a fanciful "popular uprising". This had occurred the previous evening in front of the theatre where the Beatles were performing. (For the records, the uprising had been caused by no more than about twenty girls, who were not even screaming). From that moment on, a constant stream of articles began appearing. They magnified the power of these boys from Liverpool who were capable of unleashing the primordial instincts in teenagers, yet who were also "nice" and who "washed" as one journalist from the *Daily* reported.

Towards the end of the year, a couple of quite important things occurred. The first one that the Author would like to highlight was McCartney's confession to a journalist during an interview:

D. *What about your Hofner violin-shaped bass? Is it heavy to wear onstage?*
R. No, it's light.
D. *Are violin-shaped basses more expensive than regular ones?*
R. Only 52 guineas. I'm a *skinflint*, you see.

In 1963 the market for publicity photos bearing the Beatles' autographs reached dizzying heights. There were dozens and dozens of companies churning out products that had no authorisation whatsoever from the band.

RINGO STARR

To this day, this response remains the most honest reply that McCartney ever gave to a journalist. The second event was that the band went on its first tour, from 24 to 29 October in Sweden.

On 22 November, EMI, ever faithful to the adage dear to all record companies ("Sell, before it's too late"), released a second album, *With the Beatles*.

On 4 November the Beatles performed before the Queen Mother and Princess Margaret during the Royal Variety Performance. Brian was panic-stricken when just before they were to go onstage, John decided the time had come to ruin the party. He solemnly went over to the other three Beatles who were discussing the coming engagements with Brian and according to legend told them that before their last song he would ask the audience seated in the most expensive seats (including the Royal Box with the Queen Mother and the Queen's sister) to "rattle their f- jewelry...". Only a mind with infinite powers could even begin to imagine what happened next. The other three Beatles, seized with terror, were speechless. Brian pleaded with John, looking him deep into the eyes, begging him to not do anything of the sort. The journalists the next day would have blasted them. John gave a cool look of superiority to all and, without replying, walked stiffly out of the dressing rooms towards the stage.

At that point Brian was in a mental state approaching delirium. In a last desperate attempt, he begged Paul to stop John. Paul, together with George and Ringo, hurried after Lennon who had already taken his place behind the closed curtain.

Just as in the most classic comedies, there was no time to say a word, the show was to go on. The Beatles hit the first notes of *From Me to You* behind the closed curtain, the audience started to applaud in recognition, the curtain was raised and... the future of the Beatles at that point was entirely in the hands of John Lennon.

Little by little as the end of their performance drew nearer, cold sweat began to stream down the backs of Paul, George and Ringo — and Brian's too, who was probably already contemplating immigrating to New Zealand under a false name.

At the decisive moment when John had threatened to make the fatal announcement, he went up to the microphone: "For our last number I'd like to ask your help. Would the people in the cheaper seats clap your hands? And the rest of you, if you'll just rattle your jewelry", ending his words with a smile, as if to say "I really did it this time".

In response to his words, a thunder of applause broke out, the cameras turned to focus on the Royal Box where everyone was smiling, amused at what John had just said, and applauding. The Queen Mother waved towards the stage. An extraordinary success. The next day, the newspapers greeted the Beatles proclaiming them the new messiahs, though Brian's heart might not have been as convinced at all of the goodness of John's idea.

The day after John's daredevil stunt, Brian left for New York. There, struggling with a thousand difficulties, he managed to organise a series of shows and two television appearances, on 9 and 16 February, on the "Ed Sullivan Show". The Beatles' appearances on this sacrosanct American entertainment programme turned out to be the winning move.

The most important consequence was to transform the Beatles into a global phenomenon. Yet perhaps no less significantly, it has allowed the Author of this book to finally put down his pen, having reached the stated destination of his work...

In all honesty, Brian was not exactly endowed with the most brilliant business acumen. Indeed it was precisely during this period that he laid the foundations for what would be one of the Beatles' worst deals. This could all be summed up in one word: "Seltaeb".

The word "Seltaeb", as the cleverest readers might have noted, is none other than "Beatles" spelled backwards. In actual fact, unfortunately, it was also a company created ad hoc by a group of young businessmen to whom Brian ceded the rights for the exploitation of the Beatles image in the United States.

One can just imagine the astonishment of one of the Seltaeb shareholders, Nicky Byrne, when he heard Brian's representatives ask him, "What percentage do you want?" And, when Byrne jotted down the first figure that crossed his mind, "90%" (!), how this surprise turned to speechless disbelief when no one, not even Brian's lawyer, present at the meeting, questioned this proposal.

This issue was only resolved in August 1967, following a 22 million dollar lawsuit between Brian's company NEMS and Byrne. In the meantime tens of millions of dollars were thrown out of the window and from the Beatles' pockets. The world's worst deal ever in the history of show business.

After this stroke of genius, Brian nevertheless managed to organise the Beatles' first tour in the U.S. and their appearances on the coveted "Ed Sullivan Show". He obtained the "extraordinary" sum of $10,000 for the two performances, one live and the other recorded.

Of course, the fee was considered extraordinary only to Epstein himself, since Ed Sullivan and Bob Precht, the producer of the show (and Sullivan's son-in-law), in fact both declared that this was the minimum amount that could be paid to anyone, even a group of complete unknowns. Apparently the yardstick of the Americans and that of Brian were not the same.

While Brian was busy thus financially ruining his protégés, the Beatles were nevertheless swept up in a whirlwind of engagements.

1 August 1963
Playhouse Theatre, St. John's Rd., Manchester.
Recording for the programme "Pop Go the
Beatles" broadcast on 27 August.
Recording for the programme "Pop Go the
Beatles" broadcast on 3 September.

2 August 1963
Liverpool, Grafton Rooms.
With the Undertakers, the Dennisons, Sonny
Webb & the Cascades, Chick Graham
& the Coasters.

3 August 1963
Liverpool, Cavern Club.
With the Escorts, Merseybeats, Roadrunners,
Sapphires, Johnny Ringo & the Colts.
The end of an era with the last concert
at the Cavern where the Beatles had performed
more than 300 times.

4 August 1963
Blackpool, Queen's Theatre.

5 August 1963
Morning
Manchester-Urmston, Abbotsfield Park,
"Urmston Show".
With Brian Poole & the Tremeloes, the
Dennisons, Johnny Martin & the Tremors.
Evening
Manchester-Urmston, Abbotsfield Park.
"A Twist and Shout Dance".
With Brian Poole & the Tremeloes, Dennisons,
Johnny Martin & the Tremors.

6 August 1963
Broadcasting of the programme "Pop Go the
Beatles" recorded on 16 July.
Presenter: Rodney Burke
Producer: Terry Henebery.
With the Swinging Blue Jeans.

The Beatles performed:
Pop Go the Beatles (show theme song)
I'm Gonna Sit Right Down and Cry (Over You)
Crying, Waiting, Hoping
Kansas City / Hey-Hey-Hey-Hey!
To Know Her Is to Love Her
the Honeymoon Song (Bound by Love)
Twist and Shout
Pop Go the Beatles (show theme song).

St. Saviour, the Springfield Ballroom.

7 August 1963
St. Saviour, the Springfield Ballroom.

8 August 1963
St. Peter Port, Candie Gardens Auditorium.

9 and 10 August 1963
St. Saviour, the Springfield Ballroom.

11 August 1963
Blackpool, ABC Theatre.

12-17 August 1963
Llandudno, Odeon Cinema. With Billy J. Kramer
& the Dakotas, Tommy Quickly.

13 August 1963
Broadcasting of the programme "Pop Go the
Beatles" recorded on 16 July.
Presenter: Rodney Burke
Producers: Terry Henebery & Ian Grant,
With the Hollies.
The Beatles performed:
Pop Go the Beatles (show theme song)
Long Tall Sally
Please Please Me
She Loves You
You've Really Got a Hold on Me
I'll Get You
I Got a Woman
Pop Go the Beatles (show theme song).

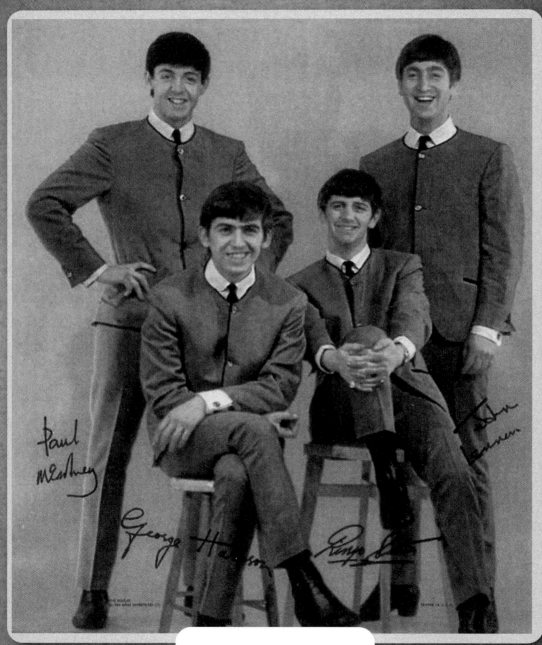

Publicity shot in 1963.

14 August 1963
TV Studio, Manchester.
Recording of the programme "Scene at 6:30"
broadcast on 19 August.

18 August 1963
TV Studio, Birmingham.
Recording of the programme "Lucky Stars
(Summer Spin)" broadcast on 24 August.
Torquay, Princess Theatre.

19 August 1963
Broadcasting of the Granada TV programme
"Scene at 6:30" recorded on 14 August.
The Beatles performed;
This Boy, Twist and Shout
I Want to Hold Your Hand.

20 August 1963
Broadcasting of the programme "Pop Go the
Beatles" recorded on 16 July.
Presenter: Rodney Burke.
Producer: Terry Henebery.
With Russ Sainty & the Nu-Notes.
The Beatles performed:
Pop Go the Beatles (theme song)
She Loves You (from the 13 August episode)
Words of Love
Glad All Over
I Just Don't Understand
(There's a) Devil in Her Heart
Slow Down
Pop Go the Beatles (show theme song).

19–24 August 1963
Bournemouth, Gaumont Cinema.
With Billy J. Kramer & the Dakotas, Tommy
Quickly.

24 August 1963
Broadcasting of the programme "Saturday Club"
recorded on 30 July.

Presenter: Brian Matthew.
Producers: Jimmy Grant & Bernie Andrews.
The Beatles performed:
Long Tall Sally
She Loves You
Glad All Over
Twist and Shout
You've Really Got a Hold on Me
I'll Get You.

Broadcasting of the programme "Lucky Stars
(Summer Spin)" recorded on 18 August.
The Beatles performed;
She Loves You
I'll Get You.

25 August 1963
Blackpool, ABC Theatre.

26-31 August 1963
Southport, Odeon Cinema.
With Gerry & the Pacemakers, Tommy Quickly.
The Beatles performed:
Roll over Beethoven
Thank You Girl
Chains
A Taste of Honey
She Loves You
Baby It's You
From Me to You
Boys
I Saw Her Standing There
Twist and Shout.

27 August 1963
Southport, Little Theatre.
Recording of the BBC-TV programme
"Mersey Sound" broadcast on 9 October and
rebroadcast on 13 November.
The Beatles performed *She Loves You.*

Broadcasting of the programme "Pop Go the Beatles" recorded on 1 August.
Presenter: Rodney Burke.
Producer: Ian Grant.
With Cyril Davies Rhythm and Blues All Stars with Long John Baldry.
The Beatles performed:
Pop Go the Beatles (show theme song).
Ooh! My Soul
Don't Ever Change
Twist and Shout
She Loves You
Anna (Go to Him)
A Shot of Rhythm and Blues
Pop Go the Beatles (show theme song).

1 September 1963
London, Teddington TV Studios.
Concert recorded by ABC TV,
broadcast on 7 September.

3 September 1963
Studio 2, BBC Aeolian Hall,
135-137 New Bond St., London.
Recording of the programme "Pop Go the Beatles" broadcast on 10 September.
Recording of the programme "Pop Go the Beatles" broadcast on 17 September.
Recording of the programme "Pop Go the Beatles" broadcast on 24 September.

Broadcasting of the programme "Pop Go the Beatles" recorded on 1 August.
Presenter: Rodney Burke
Producer: Ian Grant
With Brian Poole & the Tremeloes.
The Beatles performed:
Lucille (not broadcast)
Baby It's You (not broadcast)
She Loves You (not broadcast)
From Me to You
I'll Get You

Money (That's What I Want)
There's a Place
Honey Don't
Roll over Beethoven
Pop Go the Beatles (show theme song).

4 September 1963
Worcester, Gaumont Cinema.
With Mike Berry.

5 September 1963
Taunton, Gaumont Cinema.
With Mike Berry.

6 September 1963
Luton, Odeon Cinema.
With Mike Berry.

7 September 1963
Croydon, Fairfield Hall.
Broadcasting of the concert recorded on 1 September for ABC TV's "Big Night Out".
Just three songs were broadcast:
From Me to You
She Loves You
Twist and Shout.

Playhouse Theatre,
Northumberland Ave., London WC2.
Recording for the programme "Saturday Club" broadcast on 5 October.

8 September 1963
Blackpool, ABC Theatre.

9 September 1963
The BBC Paris Theatre, Lower Regent St., London SW1.
Recording for BBC TV.

EMI Studios – London.
Recordings for the album *With the Beatles.*

10 September 1963
Broadcasting of the programme "Pop Go the Beatles" recorded on 3 September.
Presenter: Rodney Burke
Producer: Ian Grant
With Johnny Kidd & the Pirates.
The Beatles performed:
Pop Go the Beatles (show theme song)
Too Much Monkey Business
Till There Was You
Love Me Do
She Loves You
I'll Get You
A Taste of Honey
the Hippy Hippy Shake
Pop Go the Beatles (show theme song).

12 September 1963
EMI Studios, London.
Recordings for the album *With the Beatles.*

13 September 1963
Preston, Public Hall.

14 September 1963
Northwich, Victory Memorial Hall.

15 September 1963
London, Royal Albert Hall. Great Pop Prom.
With the Rolling Stones and 12 other bands.

17 September 1963
Broadcasting of the programme "Pop Go the Beatles" recorded on 3 September.
Presenter: Rodney Burke
Producer: Ian Grant
With the Marauders.
The Beatles performed:
A Taste of Honey (not broadcast)
Pop Go the Beatles (show theme song)
Chains
You've Really Got a Hold on Me
Misery

Lucille
From Me to You
Boys
Pop Go the Beatles (show theme song).

24 September 1963
Broadcasting of the programme "Pop Go the Beatles" recorded on 3 September.
Presenter: Rodney Burke. Producer: Ian Grant.
Tony Rivers & the Castaways.
The Beatles performed:
Pop Go the Beatles (show theme song)
She Loves You
Ask Me Why
(There's a) Devil in Her Heart
I Saw Her Standing There
Sure to Fall (in Love With You)
Twist and Shout
Goodbye Jingle
Pop Go the Beatles (theme song).

4 October 1963
BBC Kingsway TV Studios, London.
Performance using playback on the programme "Ready Steady Go!" (repeat performance 31 Dec.).
The Beatles performed:
Twist and Shout
I'll Get You
She Loves You.

5 October 1963
Broadcasting of the programme "Saturday Club" recorded on 7 September.
Presenter: Brian Matthew.
Producers: Jimmy Grant & Bernie Andrews.
With the Everly Brothers.
The Beatles performed:
I Saw Her Standing There
Memphis Tennessee
Happy Birthday to You (Saturday Club)
I'll Get You
She Loves You
Lucille.

Scotland Mini-Tour

5 October 1963
Glasgow, Concert Hall.

6 October 1963
Kirkcaldy, Carlton Theatre.

7 October 1963
Dundee, Caird Hall.

End of Scotland Mini-Tour

9 October 1963
Broadcasting of the programme
"the Mersey Sound" recorded on 27 August.
The Beatles performed:
Twist and Shout (using playback)
I Saw Her Standing There
(fragment of 35 seconds)
Love Me Do (fragment of 45 seconds)
She Loves You

BBC Paris Theatre,
Lower Regent St., London SW1.
Recording for the programme "the Ken Dodd
Show" broadcast on 3 November with repeat
performance on 6 November.

11 October 1963
Trentham, Trentham Gardens Ballroom.

12 October 1963
London, NEMS offices, 13 Monmouth St.
Visit of the Beatles to the offices of the Fan Club
recorded for the show the next day on ATV.

13 October 1963
London Palladium Theatre.
Sunday Night at the London Palladium.
With Bruce Forsyth, Brook Benton, Des
O'Connor, Jack Parnell & His Orchestra, The
London Palladium Girls & Boys.
Broadcast live by ATV.

The Beatles performed:
From Me to You
I'll Get You
She Loves You
Twist and Shout.

15 October 1963
Southport, Floral Hall.

16 October 1963
Playhouse Theatre,
Northumberland Ave., London WC2.
Recording for the programme "Easy Beat"
broadcast on 20 October.

17 October 1963
EMI Studios, London.
Recording session for *With the Beatles* and for
the Christmas Special.

18 October 1963
TV Studio, Manchester.
Recording for the Granada TV programme
"Scene at 6:30" broadcast that same evening.

19 October 1963
Buxton, Pavilion Gardens Ballroom.

20 October 1963
Broadcasting of the programme "Easy Beat"
recorded on 16 October.
Presenter: Brian Matthew.
Producer: Ron Belchier.
The Beatles performed:
I Saw Her Standing There
Love Me Do
Please Please Me
From Me to You
She Loves You.

ALPHA TV Studios, Birmingham.
Recording for the programme "Thank Your
Lucky Stars" broadcast on 26 October.

21-23 October 1963
EMI Studios, London.
Recordings for the album *With the Beatles*.

Sweden Tour

24 October 1963
Karlaplansstudio, Stockholm.
Recording for the programme "Pop '63 (the
Beatles, popgrupp fran Liverpool pa besuk i
Stockholm)", broadcast on 11 November.
The Beatles performed:
Long Tall Sally
Please Please Me
I Saw Her Standing There
From Me to You
A Taste of Honey
Chains
Boys
She Loves You
Twist and Shout.

25 October 1963
Karlstad, Sundsta Laroverk, Nya aulan.
With the Phantoms.

26 October 1963
Broadcasting of the programme "Thank Your
Lucky Stars" recorded on 20 October.
The Beatles performed *She Loves You.*

Stockholm, Kungliga Hallen.

27 October 1963
Goteborg, Cirkus.

28 October 1963
Boras, Borashallen.

29 October 1963
Eskilstuna, Sporthallen.

**Poster from the Beatles' Sweden
Tour in 1963.**

30 October 1963
Karlaplansstudio, Stockholm.
Recording of the programme "Drop In"
broadcast on 3 November.

End of Sweden Tour

The Beatles Autumn Tour
With the Brook Brothers, the Rhythm & Blues
Quartet, the Vernons Girls, Peter Jay & the
Jaywalkers, the Kestrels.
The Beatles performed:
I Saw Her Standing There
From Me to You
All My Loving
You've Really Got a Hold on Me
Roll over Beethoven
Boys
Till There Was You
She Loves You
Money (That's What I Want)
Twist and Shout.

1 November 1963
Cheltenham, Odeon Cinema.

2 November 1963
Sheffield, City Hall.

3 November 1963
Leeds, Odeon Cinema.

The Beatles Autumn Tour Interrupted

3 November 1963
Broadcasting of the programme "the Ken Dodd
Show" recorded on 9 October.
Presenter: Ken Dodd
Producer: Bill Worsly
The Beatles performed *She Loves You.*

Swedish TV.
Broadcasting of the programme "Drop In"
recorded on 30 October.
The Beatles performed:
She Loves You
Twist and Shout
I Saw Her Standing There
Long Tall Sally.

4 November 1963
London, Prince of Wales Theatre.
The Royal Variety Performance.
Presenters: Dickie Henderson and Brian
Johnston. Producer: Arthur Phillips.
With Wilfrid Brambell, Harry H. Corbett, Marlene
Dietrich, Charlie Drake, Michael Flanders,
Donald Swann, Buddy Greco, Joe Loss & His
Orchestra, Susan Maughan, Nadia Nerina,
Desmond Doyle, Christopher Newton, Keith
Rosson, Ronald Plaisted, Luis Alberto del
Parana y los Paraguayos, Harry Secombe & the
"Pickwick" Company, Tommy Steele & Members
of the "Half A Sixpence" Company, Eric Sykes,
Hattie Jacques, the Clark Brothers, Francis
Brunn, the Billy Petch Dancers, Pinky & Perky,
Max Bygraves, the Prince of
Wales Theatre Orchestra.
Recorded by BBC Radio and ATV,
broadcast on 10 November.
The Beatles performed:
From Me to You
She Loves You
Till There Was You
Twist and Shout.

The Beatles Autumn Tour Resumes

5 November 1963
Slough, Adelphi Cinema.
With Peter Jay & the Jaywalkers.

6 November 1963
Northampton, ABC Cinema.

Rebroadcasting of the programme
"The Ken Dodd Show" recorded on 9 October.
Presenter: Ken Dodd.
Producer: Bill Worsly.
The Beatles performed *She Loves You.*

7 November 1963
Dublin, Adelphi Cinema.

8 November 1963
Belfast, Ritz Cinema.

Rebroadcasting of the programme
"Ready Steady Go!" of 4 October.
The Beatles performed *She Loves You.*

9 November 1963
London-East Ham, Granada Cinema.

10 November 1963
Birmingham, Hippodrome Theatre.

Broadcasting of the programme "The Royal
Command Variety Performance"
recorded on 4 November.

11 November 1963
Sveriges RP1 Channel.

Broadcasting of the programme "Pop '63 (the
Beatles, popgrupp fran Liverpool pa besuk i
Stockholm)", recorded on 24 October.
The Beatles performed:
I Saw Her Standing There
From Me to You
Money (That's What I Want)
Roll over Beethoven
You've Really Got a Hold on Me
She Loves You
Twist and Shout.

13 November 1963
Repeat of the programme "the Mersey Sound"
recorded on 27 August.

Plymouth, ABC Cinema.

14 November 1963
Exeter, ABC Cinema.

15 November 1963
Bristol, Colston Hall.

16 November 1963
Bournemouth, Winter Gardens Theatre.
Show recorded by the U.S. TV stations NBC,
ABC, and CBS.

17 November 1963
Coventry, Coventry Theatre.

19 November 1963
Wolverhampton, Gaumont Cinema.

20 November 1963
ABC Cinema, Stockport Rd.,
Manchester-Ardwick Green.
Recording for the programme
"The Beatles Come to Town".
The Beatles performed:
She Loves You, *Twist and Shout*
and *From Me to You.*

21 November 1963
Carlisle, ABC Cinema.

22 November 1963
Stockton-on-Tees, Globe Cinema.

23 November 1963
Newcastle-upon-Tyne, City Hall.

Broadcasting of the programme
"Thank Your Lucky Stars".

24 November 1963
Hull, ABC Cinema.

26 November 1963
Cambridge, Regal Cinema.

27 November 1963
York, Rialto Theatre.
Live recording for Granada TV broadcast the same day during the programme
"Scene at 6:30".
The Beatles performed *I Want to Hold Your Hand.*

28 November 1963
Lincoln, ABC Cinema.

29 November 1963
Huddersfield, ABC Cinema.

30 November 1963
Sunderland, Empire Theatre.

1 December 1963
Leicester, De Montfort Hall.

The Beatles Autumn Tour Interrupted

2 December 1963
London, Grosvenor House Hotel Ballroom.
Performance for the "Spastics Charity Show".

ATV Studios, Boreham Wood.
Recording of the programme "Morecambe & Wise Show" broadcast on 18 April 1964 and rebroadcast on 24 July.
The Beatles performed:
This Boy
I Want to Hold Your Hand
All My Loving
Moonlight Bay (with Eric Morecambe & Ernie Wise, piano Kenny Powell)

The Beatles' Autumn Tour resumed

3 December 1963
Portsmouth, Guildhall.
Recorded for Southern TV and broadcast the same day during the programme "Day by Day".

The Beatles Autumn Tour interrupted

7 December 1963
Liverpool, Empire Theatre.
Recording of the BBC programme "Juke Box Jury" broadcast the same day.
Recording of the BBC programme "Top of the Pops 1963" broadcast on 25 December.
Beatles' Northern Area Fan Club Convention Show, recorded live for BBC TV, broadcast the same day during the programme
"It's the Beatles".
The Beatles performed:
From Me to You
I Saw Her Standing There
All My Loving
Roll Over Beethoven
Boys
Till There Was You
She Loves You
This Boy
I Want to Hold Your Hand
Money (That's What I Want)
Twist and Shout
From Me to You (str.)

The Beatles Autumn Tour resumed

7 December 1963
Liverpool, Odeon Cinema.

8 December 1963
London-Lewisham, Odeon Cinema.

Poster from the Beatles' first Christmas Show in 1963.

9 December 1963
Southend-on-Sea, Odeon Cinema.

10 December 1963
Doncaster, Gaumont Cinema.

11 December 1963
Scarborough, Futurist Theatre.

12 December 1963
Nottingham, Odeon Cinema.

13 December 1963
Southampton, Gaumont Cinema.

End of The Beatles Autumn Tour

14 December 1963
London-Wimbledon,
Wimbledon Palais de Dance Ballroom.
Beatles' Southern Area Fan Club
Convention Show.
The "Chips" concert: John Lennon, seeing the
fans pressing against the protective wire fence,
declared: "If they push any harder they'll
come through as chips!".

15 December 1963
ABC TV studio, Manchester.
Recording of performance using playback
for the programme "Thank Your Lucky Stars"
broadcast on 21 December.

17 December 1963
Playhouse Theatre,
Northumberland Ave., London WC2.

1963

In these publicity shots,
the faces of Paul and Ringo
have been retouched
in a garish and artless way.

Recording of the programme "Saturday Club" broadcast on 21 December.

18 December 1963
BBC Paris Theatre,
Lower Regent St., London SW1.
Recording for the programme "From Us to You" broadcast on 26 December.

20 December 1963
Recording for the Granada TV programme "Scene at 6:30" broadcast the same day.
The Beatles performed *This Boy*.

21 December 1963
Broadcasting of the programme "Saturday Club" recorded on 17 December.
Presenter: Brian Matthew.
Producers: Jimmy Grant & Bernie Andrews.
The Beatles performed:
All My Loving
This Boy
All I Want for Christmas is a Bottle
I Want to Hold Your Hand
Till There Was You
Roll over Beethoven
Santa Claus Is Coming to Town
She Loves You.

Chrimble Muddley
Love Me Do (0:06)
Please Please Me (0:07)
From Me to You (0:07)
She Loves You (0:06)
I Want to Hold Your Hand (0:06)
Rudolph, the Red Nosed Reindeer (0:06).

Broadcasting of the programme "Thank Your Lucky Stars" recorded on 15 December.
The Beatles performed:
All My Loving
Twist and Shout
She Loves You
I Want to Hold Your Hand.

21 December 1963
Bradford, Gaumont Cinema,
The Beatles Christmas Show.
First preview concert without cabaret show.

22 December 1963
Liverpool, Empire Theatre.
Second preview concert without cabaret show.

22-29 December 1963
A documentary in colour entitled *the Beatles Come to Town*, produced by Pathe British News and recorded on 20 November, was shown in cinemas.

24-26-27-28-30-31 December 1963
Concerts and appearances.
The Beatles performed:
Roll Over Beethoven
All My Loving
This Boy
I Wanna Be Your Man
She Loves You
Till There Was You
I Want to Hold Your Hand
Money (That's What I Want)
Twist and Shout.
The Beatles also staged the sketch of the 'Courageous Railway Worker'.

26 December 1963
Broadcasting of the programme "From Us to You" recorded on 18 December.
Presenter: Rolf Harris
Producer: Bryant Marriott
The Beatles performed:
From Us to You (show theme song)
She Loves You
All My Loving
Roll over Beethoven
Till There Was You
Boys

Money (That's What I Want)
I Saw Her Standing There
Tie Me Kangaroo Down, Sport (with Rolf Harris)
I Want to Hold Your Hand
From Us to You (show theme song).

31 December 1963
Rebroadcasting of the programme
"Ready Steady Go!"
broadcast on 4 October.

And finally... the Beatles, after the umpteenth whirlwind of engagements at home, left for a series of concerts in France. While in Paris, they received news that *I Want to Hold Your Hand* had hit first place on the sales charts in the United States.

On 7 February, the band arrived in the U.S.A. for their first tour there but... that is another story or, rather, it is The Story of How the Beatles Made History, and one that many have liked to tackle. The date of 31 December 1963, however, brought the Beatles' "Prehistory" to a close. It was the era that had all begun in 1956. It was the story of the Beatles when they were still "common mortals".

Indeed, from the moment the Beatles' plane landed in New York and they set foot on the ground, it was a leap on a path that led straight into the realm of Myth.

The record *I Want to Hold Your Hand*.

Conclusion
The Beatles and the Sixties: created and creators

Love, love me do / You know I love you / I'll always be true / So please, love me do / Whoa, love me do / Someone to love / Somebody new / Someone to love / Someone like you

If any singer just starting out tried to interest a record company with a song like the above, they would probably be shown the door at best. By this we do not mean that lyrics today are better or have more intellectual aspirations than *Love Me Do*, but at least they try to hide beneath a cultural veneer with remarks such as "It's very profound, it's just that you don't understand..."

And it is precisely this complete lack of cultural pretense that characterized the Beatles' music, at least up to a certain point, until the release of *Help!* The Beatles were four nice young lads that any average British or American parent would have been overjoyed to have as their son-in-law (though without the cry of "sex, drugs and rock'n'roll" of the pop music scene...).

So that was the secret! Here, in our opinion, was the key that hundreds of critics for more than forty years got completely backwards. Indeed, it was not the Beatles who created the sixties, but rather the sixties that created the Beatles! (With the immense help of Sir George Martin on the musical side, and Brian Epstein for image making). "We were the biggest bastards on earth..." John Lennon had once said. Without going that far, let us simply say that the Beatles had a great opportunity and they took very good advantage of it, no more or less than any other boy band, as they are called today, would have done.

And it was there, on that level that, bang! Genius exploded! A boy band of today lives off the success it has accumulated. The Beatles "used" the success they had created and became The Beatles, the four most famous musicians in all the history of music. They were created by the sixties, and then they created all the rest!

Indeed nothing would ever be the same after the Beatles. Music, fashion, thinking, everything was transformed by the "creations" of the Fab Four from Liverpool. It was a perfect synergy of four minds, each complementing the other.

The Beatles were created, and they became creators. They began by being happy with *Love Me Do*. Yet as they continued on their path, they aimed higher and "greater"... to the universal concept of *"All You Need Is Love"*.

This picture was taken outside the Birmingham Hippodrome in 1963 when the Beatles had to be "smuggled" into the venue in the back of a police van.

Appendices

Let's jump ahead for a moment to 1964: the arrival of the Beatles in Amsterdam, welcomed by thousands of delirious fans. And just to think that only two years before, the band was having a hard time being taken seriously by record companies...

Discography
Official Studio Albums and Singles

Source: www.cs.mcgill.ca

Superscripted numbers indicate the peak position in the charts.

Official Studio Albums

UK

This is a listing of the official studio albums released in the UK by The Beatles (not including compilations and the like).

Please Please Me[#1 UK]
Label: Parlophone PMC 1202 (Mono) /
PCS 3042 (Stereo)
Released: 1963-03-22 and 1963-04-26
(Mono and stereo respectively)

With the Beatles[#1 UK]
Label: Parlophone PMC 1206 (Mono) /
PCS 3045 (Stereo)
Released: 1963-11-22

A Hard Day's Night[#1 UK]
Label: Parlophone PMC 1230 (Mono) /
PCS 3058 (Stereo)
Released: 1964-07-10

Beatles for Sale[#1 UK]
Label: Parlophone PMC 1240 (Mono) /
PCS 3062 (Stereo)
Released: 1964-12-04

Help![#1 UK]
Label: Parlophone PMC 1255 (Mono) /
PCS 3071 (Stereo)
Released: 1965-08-06

Rubber Soul[#1 UK]
Label: Parlophone PMC 1267 (Mono) /
PCS 3075 (Stereo)
Released: 1965-12-03

Revolver[#1 UK]
Label: Parlophone PMC 7009 (Mono) /
PCS 7009 (Stereo)
Released: 1966-08-05

Sgt. Pepper's Lonely Hearts Club Band[#1 UK]
Label: Parlophone PMC 7027 (Mono) /
PCS 7027 (Stereo)
Released: 1967-06-01

The Beatles #1 UK
Label: Apple / Parlophone PMC 7067-7068
(Mono) / PCS 7067-7068 (Stereo)
Released: 1968- 11-22

Yellow Submarine #3 UK
Label: Apple / Parlophone PMC 7070 (Mono)
/ PCS 7070 (Stereo)
Released: 1969-01-17

Abbey Road #1 UK
Label: Apple / Parlophone PCS 7088
Released: 1969-09-26

Let It Be #1 UK
Label: Apple / Parlophone PXS 1 (Box Set) /
PCS 7096 (Regular LP)
Released: 1970-05-08 (Box Set) /
1970-11-06 (Regular LP)

U.S.

In the United States, The Beatles albums were rearranged, retitled and remixed. Some of the U.S. releases were nearly identical to their UK counterparts, often only varying by one or two songs. Most releases contained songs that were also found on other records, which made things difficult for the American Beatles fan trying to purchase the band's entire catalog. By 1967, all U.S. releases matched the UK releases exactly.

Introducing... The Beatles #2 U.S.
Label: Vee-Jay VJLP 1062 (Mono) /
VJSR 1062 (Stereo)
Released: 1964- 01-06 and 1964-02-10
(Versions 1 and 2 respectively)

Meet the Beatles! #1 U.S.
Label: Capitol T 2047 (Mono) /
ST 2047 (Stereo)
Released: 1964-01-20

The Beatles' Second Album #1 U.S.
Label: Capitol T 2080 (Mono) /
ST 2080 (Stereo)
Released: 1964-04-10

A Hard Day's Night #1 U.S.
Label: United Artists UAL 3366 (Mono) /
UAS 6366 (Stereo)
Released: 1964-06-26

Something New #2 U.S.
Label: Capitol T 2108 (Mono) /
ST 2108 (Stereo)
Released: 1964-07-20

The Beatles' Story #7 U.S.
Label: Capitol TBO 2222 (Mono) /

STBO 2222 (Stereo)
Released: 1964-11-23

Beatles '65 #1 U.S.
Label: Capitol T 2228 (Mono) /
ST 2228 (Stereo)
Released: 1964-12-15

The Early Beatles #43 U.S.
Label: Capitol T 2309 (Mono) /
ST 2309 (Stereo)
Released: 1965-03-22

Beatles VI #1 U.S.
Label: Capitol T 2358 (Mono) /
ST 2358 (Stereo)
Released: 1965-06-14

Help! #1 U.S.
Label: Capitol MAS 2386 (Mono) /
SMAS 2386 (Stereo)
Released: 1965-08-13

Rubber Soul #1 U.S.
Label: Capitol T 2442 (Mono) /
ST 2442 (Stereo)
Released: 1965-12-06

Yesterday... and Today[#1 U.S.]
Label: Capitol T 2553 (Mono) /
ST 2553 (Stereo)
Released: 1966-06-20

Revolver[#1 U.S.]
Label: Capitol T 2576 (Mono) /
ST 2576 (Stereo)
Released: 1966-08-08

**Sgt. Pepper's Lonely Hearts
Club Band**[#1 U.S.]
Label: Capitol MAS 2653 (Mono) /
SMAS 2653 (Stereo)
Released: 1967-06-02

Magical Mystery Tour[#1 U.S.]
Label: Capitol MAL 2835 (Mono) /
SMAL 2835 (Stereo)
Released: 1967-11-27

The Beatles[#1 U.S.]
Label: Apple /Capitol SWBO 101
Released: 1968-11-25

Yellow Submarine[#2 U.S.]
Label: Apple / Capitol SW 153
Released: 1969-01-13

Abbey Road[#1 U.S.]
Label: Apple / Capitol SO 383
Released: 1969-10-01

Hey Jude[#2 U.S.]
Label: Apple / Capitol SW 385
Released: 1970-02-26

Let It Be[#1 U.S.]
Label: Apple / United Artists AR 34001
Released: 1970-05-18

Official Singles

The UK Singles Chart is compiled solely from sales figures; airplay statistics are not used. For this reason the chart positions for the UK Singles are indicated per disc, not per song.
The Billboard Hot 100 chart in the U.S. is compiled from sales *and* airplay statistics, so the individual songs on any given disc can be charted separately.

UK

MY BONNIE / THE SAINTS[#48]
(Polydor NH 66-833) • Released: 1962-01-5
(by "Tony Sheridan & The Beatles")

LOVE ME DO / P.S. I LOVE YOU[#17]
(Parlophone R4949) • Released: 1962-10-5

PLEASE PLEASE ME / ASK ME WHY[#2]
(Parlophone R4983) • Released: 1963-01-11

FROM ME TO YOU / THANK YOU GIRL[#1]
(Parlophone R5015) • Released: 1963-04-11

SHE LOVES YOU / I'LL GET YOU[#1]
(Parlophone R5055) • Released: 1963-08-23

**I WANT TO HOLD YOUR HAND /
THIS BOY**[#1] (Parlophone R5084) •
Released: 1963-11-9

**CAN'T BUY ME LOVE / YOU CAN'T DO
THAT**[#1] (Parlophone R5114) •
Released: 1964-03-20

**AIN'T SHE SWEET / IF YOU LOVE ME,
BABY**[#29] (Polydor NH 52-317) • Released:
1964-05-29 (B-Side with Tony Sheridan)

A HARD DAY'S NIGHT / THINGS WE SAID TODAY[#1] (Parlophone R5160) • Released: 1964-07-10

I FEEL FINE / SHE'S A WOMAN[#1] (Parlophone R5200) • Released: 1964-11-27

TICKET TO RIDE / YES IT IS[#1] (Parlophone R5265) • Released: 1965-04-09

HELP! / I'M DOWN[#1] (Parlophone R5305) • Released: 1965-07-23

WE CAN WORK IT OUT / DAY TRIPPER[#1] (Parlophone R5389) • Released: 1965-12-03

PAPERBACK WRITER / RAIN[#1] (Parlophone R5452) • Released: 1966-06-10

YELLOW SUBMARINE / ELEANOR RIGBY[#1] (Parlophone R5493) • Released: 1966-08-05

PENNY LANE / STRAWBERRY FIELDS FOREVER[#2] (Parlophone R5570) • Released: 1967-02-17

ALL YOU NEED IS LOVE / BABY YOU'RE A RICH MAN[#1] (Parlophone R5620) • Released: 1967-07-07

HELLO, GOODBYE / I AM THE WALRUS (Parlophone R5655) • Released: 1967-11-24

LADY MADONNA / THE INNER LIGHT[#1] (Parlophone R5675) • Released: 1968-03-15

HEY JUDE / REVOLUTION[#1] (Apple R5722) • Released: 1968-08-30

GET BACK / DON'T LET ME DOWN[#1] (Apple R5777) • Released: 1969-04-11

THE BALLAD OF JOHN AND YOKO / OLD BROWN SHOE[#1] (Apple R5786) • Released: 1969-05-30

SOMETHING / COME TOGETHER[#4] (Apple R5814) • Released: 1969-10-31

LET IT BE / YOU KNOW MY NAME (LOOK UP THE NUMBER)[#2] (Apple R5833) • Released: 1970-03-06

YESTERDAY / I SHOULD HAVE KNOWN BETTER[#8] (Parlophone R6013) • Released: 1976-03-08

BACK IN THE USSR / TWIST AND SHOUT[#19] (Parlophone R6016) • Released: 1976-06-29

SGT. PEPPER'S LONELY HEARTS CLUB BAND / WITH A LITTLE HELP FROM MY FRIENDS / A DAY IN THE LIFE[#63] (Parlophone R6022) • Released: 1978-09-30

BEATLES MOVIE MEDLEY / I'M HAPPY JUST TO DANCE WITH YOU[#7] (Parlophone R6055) • Released: 1982-05-25

LOVE ME DO / P.S. I LOVE YOU[#4] (reissue) (Parlophone R4949) • Released: 1982-11-19

BABY IT'S YOU / I'LL FOLLOW THE SUN / DEVIL IN HER HEART / BOYS[#7] (Apple R6406) • Released: 1995-03-20 (EP)

FREE AS A BIRD / CHRISTMAS TIME (IS HERE AGAIN)[#2] (Apple R6422) • Released: 1995-12-12

REAL LOVE / BABY'S IN BLACK[#4] (Apple R6425) • Released: 1996-03-04

U.S.

MY BONNIE / THE SAINTS (Decca 31382) • Released: 1962-04-23 (Tony Sheridan And The Beat Brothers)

PLEASE PLEASE ME / ASK MY WAY [sic] (Vee-Jay 498) • Released: 1963-02-25 (The Beattles)

FROM ME TO YOU[#116] **/ THANK YOU GIRL** (Vee-Jay 522) • Released: 1963-05-27

SHE LOVES YOU / I'LL GET YOU
(Swan 4152) • Released: 1963-09-16
(first release; white label)

I WANT TO HOLD YOUR HAND[#1] /
I SAW HER STANDING THERE[#14]
(Capitol 5112) • Released: 1963-12-26

SHE LOVES YOU[#1] / **I'LL GET YOU**
(Swan 4152) • Released: 1964-01-25
(second release; black label)

MY BONNIE[#26] / **THE SAINTS** (MGM 13213) •
Released: 1964-01-27

PLEASE PLEASE ME[#3] / **FROM ME TO YOU**[#41]
(Vee-Jay 581) • Released: 1964-01-30

ALL MY LOVING[#45] / **THIS BOY**
(Capitol 72144) • Released: 1964-02-08
(Canadian import)

ROLL OVER BEETHOVEN[#68] /
PLEASE MISTER POSTMAN (Capitol 72133)
• Released: 1964-02-15 (Canadian import)

TWIST AND SHOUT[#2] / **THERE'S A
PLACE**[#74] (Tollie 9001) •
Released: 1964-03-02

CAN'T BUY ME LOVE[#1] / **YOU CAN'T DO
THAT**[#48] (Capitol 5150) •
Released: 1964-03-16

DO YOU WANT TO KNOW A SECRET[#2] /
THANK YOU GIRL[#35] (Vee-Jay 587) •
Released: 1964-03-23

WHY[#88] / **CRY FOR A SHADOW** (MGM
13227) • Released: 1964-03-27
(The Beatles With Tony Sheridan)

LOVE ME DO[#1] / **P.S. I LOVE YOU**[#10]
(Tollie 9008) • Released: 1964-04-27

SIE LIEBT DICH (**SHE LOVES YOU**)[#97] /
I'LL GET YOU (Swan 4182) •
Released: 1964-05-21 (German)

SWEET GEORGIA BROWN / **TAKE OUT
SOME INSURANCE ON ME BABY**
(Atco 6302) • Released: 1964-06-01
(The Beatles With Tony Sheridan)

AIN'T SHE SWEET[#19] / **NOBODY'S CHILD**
(Atco 6308) • Released: 1964-07-06

A HARD DAY'S NIGHT[#1] / **I SHOULD
HAVE KNOWN BETTER**[#53] (Capitol 5222) •
Released: 1964-07-13

I'LL CRY INSTEAD[#25] / **I'M HAPPY JUST
TO DANCE WITH YOU**[#95] (Capitol 5234) •
Released: 1964-07-20

AND I LOVE HER[#12] / **IF I FELL**[#53] (Capitol
5235) • Released: 1964-07-20

MATCHBOX[#17] / **SLOW DOWN**[#25]
(Capitol 5255) • Released: 1964-08-24

I FEEL FINE[#1] / **SHE'S A WOMAN**[#4]
(Capitol 5327) • Released: 1964-11-23

EIGHT DAYS A WEEK[#1] / **I DON'T WANT
TO SPOIL THE PARTY**[#39] (Capitol 5371) •
Released: 1965-02-15

TICKET TO RIDE[#1] / **YES IT IS**[#46]
(Capitol 5407) • Released: 1965-04-19

HELP![#1] / **I'M DOWN**[#101] (Capitol 5476) •
Released: 1965-07-19

YESTERDAY[#1] / **ACT NATURALLY**[#47]
(Capitol 5498) • Released: 1965-09-13

WE CAN WORK IT OUT[#1] / **DAY TRIPPER**[#5]
(Capitol 5555) • Released: 1965-12-06

NOWHERE MAN[#3] / **WHAT GOES ON**[#81]
(Capitol 5587) • Released: 1966-02-21

PAPERBACK WRITER[#1] / **RAIN**[#23] (Capitol
5651) • Released: 1966-05-30

YELLOW SUBMARINE[#2] /
ELEANOR RIGBY[#11] (Capitol 5715) •
Released: 1966-08-08

PENNY LANE[#1] / **STRAWBERRY FIELDS FOREVER**[#8] (Capitol 5810) •
Released: 1967-02-13

ALL YOU NEED IS LOVE[#1] / **BABY YOU'RE A RICH MAN**[#34] (Capitol 5964) •
Released: 1967-07-17

HELLO, GOODBYE[#1] / **I AM THE WALRUS**[#56] (Capitol 2056) • Released: 1967-11-27

LADY MADONNA[#4] / **THE INNER LIGHT**[#96] (Capitol 2138) • Released: 1968-03-18

HEY JUDE[#1] / **REVOLUTION**[#12] (Apple 2276) • Released: 1968-08-26

GET BACK[#1] / **DON'T LET ME DOWN**[#35] (Apple 2490) • Released: 1969-05-05 (The Beatles with Billy Preston)

THE BALLAD OF JOHN AND YOKO[#8] / **OLD BROWN SHOE** (Apple 2531) •
Released: 1969-06-04

SOMETHING[#1] / **COME TOGETHER**[#1] (Apple 2654) • Released: 1969-10-06

LET IT BE[#1] / **YOU KNOW MY NAME (LOOK UP THE NUMBER)** (Apple 2764) •
Released: 1970-03-11

THE LONG AND WINDING ROAD[#1] / **FOR YOU BLUE** (Apple 2832) •
Released: 1970-05-11

GOT TO GET YOU INTO MY LIFE[#7] / **HELTER SKELTER** (Capitol 4274) •
Released: 1976-05-31

OB-LA-DI, OB-LA-DA[#49] / **JULIA** (Capitol 4347) • Released: 1976-06-08

SGT. PEPPER'S LONELY HEARTS CLUB BAND / **WITH A LITTLE HELP FROM MY FRIENDS**[#71] / **A DAY IN THE LIFE** (Capitol 4612) • Released: 1978-08-14

BEATLES MOVIE MEDLEY[#12] / **I'M HAPPY JUST TO DANCE WITH YOU** (Capitol 5107) •
Released: 1982-03-22

TWIST AND SHOUT[#23] / **THERE'S A PLACE** (Capitol 5624) • Released: 1986-07-23 (reissue)

BABY IT'S YOU[#67] / **I'LL FOLLOW THE SUN/ DEVIL IN HER HEART / BOYS** (Apple 58348) • Released: 1995-04-17 (EP)

FREE AS A BIRD[#6] / **CHRISTMAS TIME (IS HERE AGAIN)** (Apple 58497) •
Released: 1995-12-12

REAL LOVE[#11] / **BABY'S IN BLACK** (live) (Apple 58544) • Released: 1996-03-04

Bibliography

Miscellaneous or Various Authors (Aa.Vv.)

Beatles: A Tear-out Photobook, Oliver Books, 1993.

Beatles Recordings Decoder, Dynamo House, 1996.

Blinds and Shutters: The Photographs of Michael Cooper, Genesis/Hedley.

Die Beatles In Hamburg, Christians Druckerei & Verlag, 1996.

Imagine: A Celebration of John Lennon, Penguin Books, 1996.

Mike McCartney's Merseyside, Cornerhouse Publications, 1992.

Magic Eye No. 4, Magic Eye.

Paul McCartney's Oratorio, Festival Van Vlaanderen, 1998.

Remember: The Recollections and Photographs of Michael McCartney, Merehurst, 1992.

Rough Ride, World Tour Magazine, JAM Trading Co, 1990.

The Beatles Anthology, Seuil, 2000.

The Beatles Complete, Omnibus Press.

The Beatles Fab Four CD & Book Set, Merlin, 1996.

The Beatles: Get Back, Mondadori, 2021.

The Beatles in Tokyo, C.B.C., 1986.

The Beatles in Tokyo, Jam Publishing, 1986.

The Beatles Poster Book, Atlanta Press, 1989.

The Classic Poster Book: The Beatles, Pyramid Books, 1990.

The Complete Beatles Lyrics, Omnibus Press, 1982.

Yesterday, The Beatles & Die 60er, Haus Der Jugend, 1982.

Publications Listed by Author(s)

Adams, Mike, *Apple & Beatles Collectibles*, Perry & Perry Publ., 1991.

Aldridge Alan (ed.), *The Beatles Illustrated Lyrics*, Macdonald, 1969.

Aldrige, Alan. *The Beatles Illustrated Lyrics 2*, Delacorte Press, 1969.

Anjoorian, Jason. *The Beatles Japanese Record Guide*, Jason Press, 1994.

Antoni, Roberto. *I Beatles*, Targa italiana, Milan, 1989.

Antoni, Roberto. *Il viaggio dei cuori solitari*, Il Formichiere, 1979.

Argast, Thomas. *Beatles Song Index*, Thomas Argast, 1997.

Asher, Jane. *Eats for Treats*, BBC Books, 1990.

Asher, Jane. *Good Living at Christmas with Jane Asher*, BBC Worldwide, 1998.

Asher, Jane. *Jane Asher's Calendar of Cakes*, Claremont Books, 1995.

Asher, Jane. *Jane Asher's Fancy Dress*, Pelham Books, 1983.

Asher, Jane. *The Best of Good Living*, BBC Books, 1998.

Asher, Jane. *The Longing*, Harper Collins, 1996.

Asher, Jane. *The Question*, Harper Collins, 1998.

Asher, Jane. *Trick of the Trade*, Thorsons, 1999.

Asher, J., Einon, D. *Time to Play*, Michael Jospeh, Penguin Group, 1995.

Assagas, M., Meunier, C. The *Beatles and the Sixties*, Henry Holt Reference Books, 1996.

Assante, E., Castaldo, G., *Beatles*, Laterza, 2015

Augsburger, J., Eck, M., Rann, R. *The Beatles Memorabilia Price Guide*, Branyan Press, 1988.

Augsburger, J., Eck, M., Rann, R. *Third Edition of the Beatles Memorabilia Price Guide*, Antique Trader Books, 1997.

Avila Cruz, Alvaro. *Heroe De La Clase Trabajadora*, Universidad Autonoma del Estado de Hidalgo, 1996.

Axelrod, Mitchell. *Beatletoons: The Real Story Behind the Cartoon Beatles*, Wynn Publishing, 1999.

Aylward, John. *The Apple Singles File*, Enlighten Books.

Babiuk, Andy. *The Beatles*, Gear Backbeat Books, 2001.

Bacon, David. *The Beatles: England*, Columbus Books, 1982.

Bacon, T., Benedetto, Burrluck, Carter, *Guitar: A Complete Guide for the Player*, Balaton Outline Press, 2002.

Bacon, T., Day, P. *The Gretsch Book*, Belaton Books, 1996.

Bacon, T., Day, P. *The Rickenbacker Book*, Outline Press, 1994.

Bacon, T., Moorhouse, B. *The Bass Book*, Outline Press, 1995.

Bacon, Tony. *Electric Guitars: The Illustrated Encyclopedia*, Balaton Outline Press, 2000.

Bacon, Tony. *Fuzz & Feedback: Classic Guitar Music of the '60s*, Miller Freeman Books, 1997.

Bacon, Tony (ed.), *Classic Guitars of the Sixties*, Outline, 1997.

Badman, Keith. *Beatles off the Record*, Omnibus Press, 2000.

Badman, Keith. *The Beatles After the Break-Up*, Omnibus Press, 1999.

Baird, Julia. *John Lennon My Brother*, Grafton Books, 1988.

Bakaryov, V.V., *John Lennon, Myths and Reality*, Klyon, 1992.

Baker, Glenn A. *The Beatles Down Under*, Magnum Music Group, 1996.

Baker, Glenn A. Dilernia Roger, *The Beatles Down Under: The 1964 Australia & New Zealand Tour*, Pierian Press, 1986.

Barrell, Tony. *The Beatles on the Roof*, Omnibus Press, 2017.

Barrow, Tony. *On the Scene at the Cavern*, Tony Barrow International, 1984.

Barrow, Tony. *P.S. We Love You*, Mirror Books, 1982.

Barrow, Tony. *The Beatles in Germany*, Tracks, 1997.

Baum, Peter. *The Beatles in Tokyo 1966*, The Japan Times, 1995.

Baxter, Lew. *Allan Williams is... The Fool on the Hill*, Praxis, 2003.

BBC. The *Lennon Tapes 6/12/80*, BBC, 1980.

Beatles (The). *Anthology*, Chronicle Books, 2000.

Bedford, Carol. *Waiting for the Beatles*, Blandford Press, 1984.

Behnke, Frank. *Das Grosse Klaus Beyer – Beatles Buch*, Martin Schmitz Verlag, 1995.

Belmer, Scott. *Not for Sale*, the Hot Wax Press, 1997.

Belmo. *The Making of Sgt. Pepper*, CG Publishing, 1996.

Bennahum, David. *The Beatles after the Break-Up in Their Own Words*, Omnibus Press, 1991.

Benson, Harry. *Once There Was a Way*, Thames and Hudson, 2003.

Benson, Harry. *The Beatles Now and Then*, Universe Publ., 1998.

Benson, Joe. *Uncle Joe's Record Guide, the Beatles*, Joe Benson Unlimited, 1990.

Benson, Ross. *Paul McCartney Behind the Myth*, Gollancz, 1992.

Bergholz, A., Hallberg, C. *Beatles I Sverige*, Beatles Information Center, 1993.

Bergholz, Thielow. *30 Years of Rockin' the World: The Rattles*, Homemade, 1993.

Bernstein, S., Aaron, A. *Not Just the Beatles...*, Jacques & Flusster Publ., 2000.

Berry, Rynn. *Famous Vegetarians & Their Favorite Recipes*, Panjandrum, 1990.

Best, Pete. *Beatle! The Pete Best Story*, Plexus, 1985.

Best, P., Harry, B. *The Best Years of the Beatles*, Headline Book Publishing, 1996.

Best, Roag, Pete, Rory. *The Beatles: The True Beginnings*, Spine Screen Press, 2002.

Bezinger, Olaf. *Meisterwerke Kurz Und Bundig, Sgt Pepper Der Beatles*, Piper Verlag GMBH, 2000.

Bicknell, A., Marsh, G. *Baby, You Can Drive My Car!* Number 9 Books, 1989.

Bindervoet, E., Jan, H.R. *Help! The Beatles In Het Nederlands*, Nijgh & Van Damme, 2003.

Birkenstadt, J., Belmo. *Black Market Beatles*, Collectors Guide Publishing, 1995.

Black, Johnny. *Recording Sgt. Pepper's Tracks*, 1998.

Blake, John. *All You Needed Was Love: The Beatles after the Beatles*, Perigee Books, 1981.

Blaney John, *Paul McCartney: The Songs He Was Singing*, Paper Jukebox, 2003.

Blay, Arturo. *Paul McCartney*, Editorial La Mascara, 1997.

Blisniuk, Raul. *The Beatles Exhibition*, Produccio Graficas Integrados, 1996.

Bohm, T., Stark, J. *Die Grossen Stars Der Popmusik*, ECON Taschenbuch Verlag, 1988.

Booth, Tony. *The Beatles in Posters: A Collection of Concert Artwork by Tony Booth*, The History Press Ltd, 2017.

Bowen, Phil. *Things We Said Today*, Stride, 1995.

Braam, Willi. *Das Album Der Beatles*.

Bradman, Tony. *Profiles... John Lennon*, Hamisch Hamilton, 1985.

Brassey, Richard. *Brilliant Brits: The Beatles*, Orion Childrens Books, 2003.

Bratifisch, Rainer. *The Fab Four, Das Grosse Beatles Lexikon*, Lexikon Imprint Verlag, 2002.

Braun, Michael. *Love Me Do: The Beatles Progress*, Penguin, 1964.

Bresler, Fenton. *The Murder of John Lennon*, Sidgwick & Jackson, 1989.

Bresler, Fenton. *Who Killed John Lennon*, St. Martin, 1989.

Bromell, Nick. *Tomorrow Never Knows*, University of Chicago Press, 2000.

Bronson, Harold. *Rock Explosion: The British Invasion of America in Photos 1962-1967*, Rhino Books, 1984.

Brown, Peter. *The Love You Make*, MacMillan, 1983.

Brown, Peter. *The Love You Make: An Insider's Story of the Beatles*, Penguin Books, N.Y., 1981.

Bryan, Kelly Michael. *The Beatles Myth*, McFarland, 1991.

Burch, Regina. *Love Is All You Need*, the Chapel Hill Press, 1998.

Burrows, Terry. *John Lennon: A Story in Photographs*, Brown Patworks, 2000.

Burrows, Terry. *The Beatles*, Chartwell Books, 1996.

Burt, R., Wells, M. *Rockups: The Beatles Story*, Orbis Publishing, 1985.

Buskin, Richard. *Beatle Crazy, Memories and Memorabilia*, Salamander Books, 1994.

Buskin, Richard. *Days in the Life: The Lost Beatles Archives*, Star Publishing, 1998.

Buskin, Richard. *John Lennon, His Life and Legend*, Omnibus Press, 1991.

Buskin, Richard. *The Complete Idiot's Guide to the Beatles*, Alpha Books, 1998.

Butkus, Gunther. *Die Beatles Und Ich*, Pendragon, 1995.

Cahill, Marie, *The Beatles: A Pictorial History*, Grange & Bison Books, 1990.

Cambell, Colin, *Things We Said Today,* Pierian Press, 1980.

Capisani, A.D. (interview of), *John Lennon Canzoni e musica*, Lato Side, 1981.

Carr, Roy, *Beatles at the Movies*, UFO Music, 1996.

Carr, R., Tyler, T. *The Beatles: An Illustrated Record*, Random House, 1975.

Carwardine, Mark. *On the Trail of the Whale*, Thunder Bay Publ., 1994.

Castaldo, Gino. *Beatles e Rolling Stones. Apollinei e dionisiaci*, Einaudi, 2022.

Castleman, Harry. *All Together Now*, Pierian Press, 1976.

Castleman, Harry. *The Beatles Again?* Pierian Press, 1977.

Castleman, H., Podrazik, W.J. *The End of the Beatles?* Pierian Press, 1985.

Celsi, Theresa. *The Beatles*, Ariel Books, 1993.

Cepican, Bob. *Yesterday... Came Suddenly: The Definitive History of the Beatles*, Arbour House, 1985.

Charles, Paul. *First of the True Believers*, the Do-Not Press Ltd., 2002.

Charles, Paul. *The Beatles Pocket,* Essentials, 2003.

Clayson, Alan. *John Lennon*, Sanctuary Publishing, 2003.

Clayson, Alan. *Ringo Starr*, Sanctuary Publishing, 2001.

Clayson, Alan., *Ringo Starr – Straight Man or Joker?* Sidgwick & Jackson, 1991.

Clayson, Alan. *The Cradle of British Rock*, Hamburg Sanctuary Publishing, 1997.

Clayson, Alan. *The Quiet One: A Life of George Harrison*, Sidwick & Jackson, 1990.

Clayson, A., Leigh, S. *The Walrus Was Ringo – 11 Beatles Myths Debunked*, Chrome Dreams, 2003.

Clayson, A., Sutcliffe, P. *Stuart Sutcliffe: The Lost Beatle*, Pan Books, 1994.

Clayton, M., Thomas, G. *John Lennon Unseen Archives*, Parragon, 2002.

Clifford Mike, *The Beatles,* Smithmark Publ., 1992.

Coates, Tim. *John Lennon: The FBI Files*, Littlehampton Book Services, 2003.

Cohen, Sara. *Rock Culture in Liverpool*, Oxford University Press, 1991.

Coleman, Ray. *Brian Epstein: The Man Who Made the Beatles*, Viking Book, 1989.

Coleman, Ray. *John Lennon 1940/1980*, Pavilion Books, 1981.

Coleman, Ray. *John Ono Lennon*, Sidgwick & Jackson, 1984.

Coleman, Ray. *John Winston Lennon Vol. 1, 1940-1966*, Sidgwick & Jackson, 1984.

Coleman, Ray. *Lennon*, McGraw Hill, 1984.

Coleman, Ray. *Lennon: The Definitive Biography,* Harper Perennial, N.Y., 1992.

Coleman, Ray. *McCartney Yesterday & Today*, Boxtree, 1995.

Collard, K., Bregoli, J. *In the Hollows*, Namaste Publications, 1987.

Connolly, Ray. *Stardust Memories*, Pavilion, 1983.

Conord, Bruce W. *Pop Culture Legends: John Lennon*, Chelsea House Publishers, 1994.

Corbin, Carole Lynn. *Lennon*, Franklin Watts, 1984.

Cording R., Jankowski-Smith, S., Miller, E. *In My Life (Encounters with the Beatles)*, International Publishing, 1998.

Coren, G., Sinclair, D. *The Beatles: Free as a Bird*, UFO Music, 1995.

Cott, Jonathan. *Get Back*, Apple, 1970.

Cox, P., Lindsay, J. *Official Price Guide to the Beatles*, House of Collectables, 1995.

Cox, P., Lindsay, J. *The American Price Guide for American Records*, Perry Cox Ent., 1992.

Croft, Andrew. *Collecting Beatles Sheet Music & Songbooks*, Beatology, 2003.

Crusells, M., Iranzo, A. *The Beatles: Una Filmografía Musical*, Royal Books, 1995.

Daggett, Peter. *The Summer of 1968: The Mad Day Out*, Tracks, 1996.

Dailey, Forrest. *The Fifth Magician*, 1st Books, 2003.

Davies, Hunter. *The Beatles*, McGraw Hill, 1985.

Davies, Hunter. *The Beatles Book*, Ebury Publishing, 2019.

Davies, Hunter. *The Beatles: The Authorised Biography*, Ebury Publishing, 2009.

Davies, Hunter. *The Quarrymen*, Omnibus Press, 2001.

Davis, Andy. *Sir Paul McCartney*, Tracks, 1997.

Davis, Andy. *The Beatles Files*, Bramley Books, 1998.

Davis, Arthur. *The Beatles Quote Unquote*, Parragon, 1994.

de Castro Fresnadillo J., Sanchez, Romero E. *Ole Beatles*, Pages Editors, 1994.

de Miguel, Maurilio. *The Beatles El Libro*, Luca Editorial S.A., 1994.

Delano, Julia. *The Beatles Album*, Grange Books, 1991 [Delano, Julia. *Les Beatles : Une Photobiographie*, Presses de la Cité, 1993].

Delbuono, R., Delbuono, C. *The Beatles: A Collection*, Robcin Associates, 1982.

DeWitt, Howard A., *Paul McCartney: From Liverpool to Let It Be*, Horizon Books, 1992.

Di Franco, Philip. *A Hard Day's Night*, Chelsea House, 1977.

Di Lello, Richard. *The Longest Cocktail Party*, Charisma Books, 1973.

Dieckmann, Ed. *Made In Holland*, Franck Leenheer Records, 1996.

Dieckmann, Ed. *Made in Holland Too*, Franck Leenheer Records, 1997.

Dister, Alain. *Les Beatles*, Albin Michel, 1981.

Dister, Alain. *Los Beatles*, Jucar, 1994.

Doggett, Peter. *Classic Rock Albums Series, Abbey Road / Let It Be: The Beatles*, Schirmer Books, 1998.

Domnitz, Linda "Deer". *John Lennon: Conversations*, Coleman Publishing, 1984.

Doney, Malcom. *Lennon & McCartney*, Midas Books, 1981.

Dorough, Prince. *Popular Music Culture in America*, Ardley House, 1992.

Dowlding, William. *Beatlesongs*, Simon & Schuster, 1989.

Doyle, Tom. *Man on the Run: Paul McCartney in the 1970s*, Random House, 2014.

Du Noyer, Paul. *Liverpool, Wondrous Place*, Virgin Books, 2002.

Du Noyer, Paul. *We All Shine On*, Carlton Books, 1997.

Dunn, Joe. *Hofner Violin "Beatle" Bass*, New Cavendish Books, 1996.

Eliott, Anthony. *The Mourning of John Lennon*, University of California Press, 1999.

Elson, Howard. *McCartney Songwriter*, Comet Books, 1986.

Engelhardt, Kristofer. *Beatles Undercover*, Collectors Guide Publishing, 1998.

English, D., Brychta, J. *The Bunbury's - Bun Noel*, Harper Collins, 1989.

Epstein, Brian. *A Cellar Full of Noise*, New English Library, 1981.

Erlemann, Kurt. *30 Years of Beatles Music: A Chronicle*, Er-Ro Publications, 1987.

Erlewine, M., Bogdanov, V., Woodstra, C. *All Music Guide to Rock*, Miller Freeman Books, 1995.

Eppridge, Bill. *The Beatles: Six Days That Changed the World*, Universe Publishing, 2016.

Evans, Mike. *In the Footsteps of the Beatles*, Merseyside County Council, 1981.

Evans, Mike. *The Art of the Beatles*, Beech Tree Books, 1984.

Everett, Walter. *The Beatles as Musicians*, Oxford University Press, 1999.

Ewing, John. *The Beatles*, Orion/Carlton Books, 1994.

Fast, Julius. *The Beatles: The Real Story*, Putnam, 1968.

Featherstone-Witty, Mark. *Optimistic Even Then*, SPA Press, 2001.

Fein, Art. *The Greatest Rock & Roll Stories*, General Publishing Group, 1996.

Fenick, Barbara. *Collecting the Beatles*, Pierian Press, 1985.

Fenick, Barbara. *Collecting the Beatles: Volume 2*, Pierian Press, 1987.

Ferguson, A., Bicknell, A., *Ticket to Ride: The Ultimate Beatles Tour Diary!*, Glitter Books, 1998.

Ferrari, Lillie. *The Girl from Norfolk with the Flying Table*, Michael Joseph, 1996.

Flippo, Chet. *McCartney: The Biography*, Sidwick & Jackson, 1988.

Foster, Ron. *Pure Gold Rock & Roll Trivia Questions*, Historical Publications, 1995.

Fox, Ted. *Showtime at the Apollo*, Q Quartet, 1983.

Frame, Pete. *The Beatles and Some Other Guys*, Omnibus Press, 1997.

Freeman, Robert. *Fotografias/Fotografies*, Universitat de Lleida, 2002.

Freeman, Robert. *The Beatles: A Private View*, Octopus, 1960.

Friede, G., Titone, R., Weiner. S. *The Beatles A to Z*, Methuen, 1980.

Friedman, Rick. *Beatles Words Without Music*, Grosset, 1968.

Frietsch, Christian. *Paul McCartney: Conversation for Europe*, Radio Victoria, 1992.

Fulpen, H.V. *Beatles: An Illustrated Diary*, Plexus, 1983.

Fumiya, Saimaru Nishi. *The John Lennon Family Album*, Chronicle Books, 1990.

Furedi, Judith. *Dear John*, Lucky and Me Productions, 2002.

Gaar, Gillian G. *She's a Rebel: The History of Women in Rock & Roll*, Seal Press, 1992.

Gambaccini, Paul. *Paul McCartney in His Own Words*, Omnibus Press, 1976.

Garbarini, Vic. *Strawberry Fields Forever: John Lennon Remembered*, Bantam, 1980.

Gardiner, Juliet. *From the Bomb to the Beatles*, Collins & Brown, 1999.

Garner, Paul. *The Beatles in London Walk*, Louis London Walks, 1999.

Garry, Len. *John, Paul and Me Before the Beatles*, Collectors Guide Publishing, 1997.

Geller, Debbie. *The Brian Epstein Story*, Faber and Faber, 2000.

Gelly, Dave. *The Facts About a Pop Group Featuring Wings*, Deutsch, 1977.

Gentle, J., Forsyth I. *First Ever Tour, Johnny Gentle & The Beatles, Scotland 1960*, Merseyrock Publications, 1998.

Geringer, Ken. *Nobody Told Me*, Hipway Press, 2002.

Gilbert, Judith. *Born for Chinchilla*, Verlag Ulrich Martzinek, 1991.

Giuliano, G. & B. *The Lost Beatles Interviews*, Virgin, 1995.

Giuliano, Geoffrey. *Blackbird : The Unauthorized Biography of Paul McCartney*, Smith Gryphon, 1991.

Giuliano, Geoffrey. *Dark Horse: The Secret Life of George Harrison*, Bloomsbury Publishing, 1989.

Giuliano, Geoffrey. *Lennon in America*, Cooper Square Press, 2000.

Giuliano, Geoffrey. *The Beatles: A Celebration*, Methuen, 1992.

Giuliano, Geoffrey. *The Illustrated George Harrison*, Sunburst Books, 1993.

Giuliano, Geoffrey. *The Illustrated John Lennon*, Sunburst Books, 1993.

Giuliano, Geoffrey. *The Illustrated Paul McCartney*, Sunburst Books, 1993.

Giuliano, Geoffrey. *Tomorrow Never Knows*, Paper Tiger, 1991.

Giuliano, Geoffrey. *Two of Us: Lennon & McCartney Behind the Myth*, Penguin Putnam, 1999.

Giuliano G., Devi V. *Glass Onion: The Beatles in Their Own Words*, Da Capo Press, 2000.

Giuliano G., Giuliano, B. *The Lost Lennon Interviews*, Adams Media Corporation, 1996.

Giuliano G., Giuliano, B. *Things We Said Today: Conversations with The Beatles*, Adams Media Corp., 1998.

Goldman, Albert. *The Lives of John Lennon*, William Morrow, N.Y., 1988.

Goldmine Magazine (ed.). *The Beatles Digest*, Krause Publications, 2000.

Goldmine Magazine (ed.). *The Beatles Digest – 2nd Edition*, Krause Publications, 2002.

Goldsmith, Martin. *The Beatles Come to America*, John Wiley & Sons, 2004.

Goodgold, Edwin. *The Complete Beatles Quiz Book*, Warner Books, 1983.

Gottfridsson, Hans Olaf. *The Beatles from Cavern to Star-Club*, Premium Publishing, 1997.

Gottfridsson, Hans Olaf. *Tony Sheridan with the Beatles – Beatles Bop – Hamburg Days*, Bear Family Records, 2001.

Granados, Stefan. *Those Were the Days*, Cherry Red Books, 2002.

Grandfils, Dominique. *Paul McCartney*, Zelie, 2001.

Grasso, Rosario. *The Beatles in Italy*, Edizioni Dafni, 1981.

Green, John. *Dakota Days*, St. Martin Press, 1983.

Greenwald, Ted. *30 Jaar the Beatles*, Ars Scribendi, 1993.

Greenwald, Ted. *The Beatles Companion*, Smithmark Pub., 1992.

Gross, Edward. *McCartney: 20 Years on His Own*, Pioneer Books, 1990.

Grove, Martin. *Beatle Madness*, Manor Books, 1978.

Gruen, B., Mieses S. *Listen to These Pictures: Photographs of John Lennon*, Morrow Books, 1985.

Gunther, Curt, *Mania Days*, Genesis Publications, 2000.

Hamilton, Alan. *Paul McCartney*, Hamish H., 1983.

Harrison, George. *I, Me, Mine*, Simon & Schuster, 1980.

Harry, Bill. *Ask Me Why: The Beatles Quiz Book*, Javelin Books, 1985.

Harry, Bill. *Beatlemania: An Illustrated Filmography Vol. 4*, Virgin Books, 1984.

Harry, Bill. *Beatlemania: The History of the Beatles on Film*, Avon, 1985.

Harry, Bill. *Beatles for Sale: The Beatles Memorabilia Guide*, Virgin Books, 1985.

Harry, Bill. *Mersey Beat: The Beginnings of the Beatles*, Omnibus Press, 1977.

Harry, Bill. *Paperback Writers: The History of the Beatles in Print*, Virgin Books, 1984.

Harry, Bill. *the Beatles Encyclopedia, Revised and Updated*, Virgin, 2000.

Harry, Bill. *The Beatles for Sale: The Beatles Memorabilia Guide*, Virgin Books, 1985.

Harry, Bill. *The Beatles: Paperback Writers Vol. 3*, Avon Books, 1984.

Harry, Bill. *The Beatles Who's Who*, Aurum, 1982.

Harry, Bill. *The Beatles: An Illustrated Filmography*, Virgin Books, 1984.

Harry, Bill. *The Book of Beatle Lists*, Javelin Books, 1985.

Harry, Bill. *The Book of Lennon*, Delilah comm., 1984.

Harry, Bill. *The Encyclopedia of Beatles People*, Blandford/Cassell Plc., 1997.

Harry, Bill. *The John Lennon Encyclopedia*, Virgin Publications, 2000.

Harry, Bill. *The Ultimate Beatles Encyclopedia*, Virgin, 1992.

Harry, Bill. *The British Invasion*, Chrome Dreams, 2004.

Harry, Bill. *The McCartney File*, Virgin Books, 1986.

Harry, Bill. *The Paul McCartney Encyclopedia*, Virgin Books, 2002.

Hasabe, Koh, *The Beatles 1965/1966/1967*, Shinko Music, 1996.

Haskell, B. Hanhardt, J. *Yoko Ono, Arias and Objects*, Gibbs Smith, 1991.

Hately, David. *Paul McCartney's Rupert and the Frog Song*, Ladybird Books, 1986.

Headon, Sean. *The Totally 100% Unofficial Beatles Poster Book*, Granddreams, 1999.

Heatley, Michael. *The Immortal John Lennon*, Longmeadow, 1992.

Henke, James. *Lennon His Life and Work*, The Rock and Roll Hall of Fame, 2000.

Henke, J., Ono Y. *Lennon Legend*, Chronicle Books, 2003.

Henning, E. E., Bing, J. *Det Myke*, Landskapet, 1977.

Hertsgaard, Mark. *A Day in the Life, the Music and Artistry of the Beatles*, MacMillan, 1995.

Herzogenrath, W., Hansen, D. *John Lennon: Zeichnungen, Performance, Film*, Cantz Verlag, 1995.

Heylin, Clinton. *The Great White Wonders: A History of Rock Bootlegs*, Viking, 1993.

Hibbert, Tom. *The Best of Q: Who the Hell...?*, Virgin, 1994.

Hieronimus, Robert R. *Inside the Yellow Submarine*, Krause Publications, 2002.

Higgs, John. *Love and Let Die: Bond, the Beatles and the British Psyche*, Orion Publishing Co., 2022.

Hill, T., Clayton M. *The Beatles Unseen Archives*, Paragon Books, 2001.

Hipgnosis. *Hands across the Water: Wings Tour USA*, Paper Tiger, 1978.

Hockinson, Michael J. *Nothing is Beatleproof*, Popular Culture, 1990.

Hockinson, Michael J. *The Ultimate Beatles Quiz Book II*, St. Martin's Griffin, 2000.

Hoffmann, Dezo. *The Beatles Conquer America*, HarperCollins, 1985.

Hoffmann, Dezo. *With the Beatles*, Omnibus Press, 1982.

Hoffmann D., Jopling, N. *John Lennon*, Columbus Books, 1985.

Hopkins, Jerry. *Yoko Ono: A Biography*, Sidgwick & Jackson, 1987.

Hörig, Elmar. *Beatles Story*, Eichborn Verlag Ag, 1994.

Howard, John. *The Beatles Unseen*, Penguin Books, 1996.

Howlett, Kevin. *The Beatles at the BEEB*, BBC Books, 1982.

Howlett, Kevin. *The Beatles: The BBC Archives: 1962-1970*, Ebury Publishing, 2015.

Howlett, K., Lewisohn, M. *In My Life: John Lennon Remembered*, BBC Books, 1990.

Humphries, Patrick. *The Beatles (Vol. 2)*, Omnibus Press, 1998.

Huntley, Elliot J. *Behind That Locked Door*, Xerostar Holdings, 2002.

Hurta, Carvalho Eide H. *O Pensamento Vivo De John Lennon*, Martin Cleret Editores, 1987.

Hutchins, C., Thompson P. *Elvis Meets the Beatles*, Smith Gryphon Publ., 1994.

Huyette, Marcia. *John Lennon: A Real Live Fairytale*, Hidden Studio, 1982.

Ichbiah, Daniel. *Et Dieu créa les Beatles*, Paris, Les Cahiers de l'info, 2009.

Ingham, Peter. *The Beatles Discography: The Complete Illustrated Discography of the Beatles in Japan*, Shinko Music, 1986.

Insolera, Massimo. *Paul McCartney*, Arcana, 1979.

Iodice, F., Paoli G. *Beatles 14 Anni Di Show*, Fratelli Gallo Editori, 1985.

Iranzo, A.. Vizcarra A. *Las Canciones Secretas De Los Beatles*, Editorial Milenio, 2002.

Jacobson, Laurie. *Top of the Mountain: The Beatles at Shea Stadium 1965*, Hal Leonard Corporation, 2022.

Jaspèer, Tony. *Paul McCartney & Wings*, Octopus Books, 1977.

Jones, David. *Beatles in Wales*, St. David's Press, 2002.

Jones, Ron. *The Beatles Liverpool: The Definitive Guide*, Glasgow and Associates, Preston, 1991.

Jouffa, François. *McCartney 50 Ans*, Michel Lafon, 1993.

Kabluechko, Y. *The Beatles Yeah! Yeah! Yeah!*, T/O Dialog, 1995.

Kane, Larry, *Ticket to Ride*, Running Press Books Publ., 2003.

Kartavykh, A.E., *English Is Easy*, Moscovsky Litzey, 1995.

Kaufman, Murray, *Murray the K Tell It Like It Is Baby*, Eden, 1966.

Kay, Hillary. *Rock'n'Roll Collectables: An Illustrated History of Rock Memorabilia*, Pyramid Books.

Kaye, Peter. *Beatles in Liverpool*, Starlit, 1987.

Kazinn, Allan. *The Beatles*, Phaidon Press, 1995.

Keen, Linda. *John Lennon in Heaven*, Pan Publishing, 1993.

Kendall, Brian. *Our Hearts Went Boom: the Beatles Invasion of Canada*, Viking/Penguin Books, 1997.

King, L.R.E. *Do You Want to Know a Secret?* Storyteller Productions, 1988.

King, L.R.E. *Fixing a Hole*, Storyteller Productions, 1989.

King, L.R.E. *Unfinished Music No.1*, Storyteller Productions, 1988.

King, L.R.E. *Unfinished Music No.2*, Storyteller Productions, 1992.

Kirchherr, Astrid. *When We Was Fab*, Genesis Publications, 2003.

Kirkpatrick, Jim. *Before He Was Fab*, Cache River Press 2000.

Kite, M.R. *Cancelled! The Beatles Unreleased*

Recordings, Soundbit Verlag, 1995.

Knight, Judson. *Abbey Road to Zapple Records*, Taylor Publishing Company, 1999.

Krauth, Connie. *Destined for Greatness: The Beatles and Me*, Say the Word, 1994.

Kruger, Ulf. *Beatles Guide Hamburg*, Europa Verlag, 2001.

Kruger, Ulf. *The Many Faces of John Lennon*, K&K, 2000.

Laing, D., Josephs N. *Popular Music*, Cambridge Library Press, 1987.

Lange, Larry. *The Beatles Way: Fab Wisdom for Everyday Life*, Beyond Words Publishing, 2001.

Lansky, Thomas F., *Paul McCartney*, Moewig Rastatt, 1988.

Lari, Emilio. *The Beatles: Photographs from the Set of Help!*, Universe Publishing, 2015.

Leach, Sam. *Follow the Merseybeat Road*, Eden, Liverpool, 1978.

Leach, Sam. *The Rocking City: The Explosive Birth of the Beatles*, Pharaoh Press, 1999.

Leach. S., Matthews, D. *Les Beatles avant la gloire*, Rouchon, 2007.

Lefcowitz, Eric. *Tomorrow Never Knows: The Beatles' Last Concert*, Terra Firma Books, 1987.

Leigh, Spencer. *Brother Can You Spare a Rhyme*, Spencer Leigh, 2000.

Leigh, Spencer. *Drummed Out! The Sacking of Pete Best*, Northdown Publishing, 1998.

Leigh, Spencer. *Let's Go Down the Cavern*, Vermilion Hutchinson, 1984.

Leigh, Spencer. *Puttin' on the Style: The Lonnie Donegan Story*, Finbarr International, 2003.

Leigh, Spencer. *Sweeping the Blues Away*, IPM, 2002.

Leigh, Spencer. *Speaking Words of Wisdom: Reflection on the Beatles*, Cavern City Tours, Liverpool, 1991.

Leigh, Spencer. *The Best of Fellas: The Story of Bob Wooler*, Drivegreen Publications, 2002.

Leigh, Vanora. *Great Lives: John Lennon*, Wayland, 1986.

Le Mesurier, R., Honeyman-Scott P. S. *Rock'n'Roll Cuisine*, Aurum Press, 1988.

Lennon, Cynthia. *A Twist of Lennon*, Star Books, 1978.

Lennon, John. *A Spaniard in the Works*, Canongate Books Ltd , 2014.

Lennon, John. *In His Own Write*, Canongate Books Ltd, 2014.

Lennon, John. *John Lennon Amor Verdadero, Dibujos Para Sean*, Destino, 2000.

Lennon, John. *John Lennon: Dessins pour Sean*, Hors Editions, 2000.

Lennon, John. *Real Love: The Drawings for Sean*, Random House, 1999.

Lennon, John. *Skywriting by Word of Mouth*, Pan Books, 1987.

Lennon, John. *The John Lennon Letters*, Little, Brown & Company, 2013.

Lennon, John. *The Penguin John Lennon*, Penguin, 1966.

Lennon, John. *Zwei Jungfrauen Oder Wahnsinnig In Danemark*, Pendragon, 1993.

Lennon, J., Marchbank, P., Miles, B. *John Lennon in His Own Words*, Music Sales Corp., 1990.

Lennon, J., Ono, Y., Gruen, B. *John Lennon: Sometime in New York City*, Genesis Publications, 1995.

Lennon, Pauline. *Daddy Come Home: The True Story of John Lennon and His Father*, Angus & Robertson, 1990.

Leonard, Hal. *The Complete Beatles*, Hal Leonard P., USA, 1988.

Leopold, F., Planker, Z. *Servus Beatles*, Lowen Edition, 1995.

Lesueur, Daniel. *Les Beatles : La discographie définitive*, Éditions Alternatives, 1997.

Lev, Doctor. *Billy Shears!* Dorrance Publishing Co., 2001.

Levy, Jeffrey. *Apple Log IV*, MonHunProd Group, 1990.

Levy, Jeffrey. *The Apple Records References Vol. 1-3*, the Apple Log, 1992.

Lewis, Vic. *Music and Maiden Overs (My Show Business Life)*, Chatto and Windus, 1987.

Lewis, M., Spignesi, S.J. *100 Best Beatles Songs: A Passionate Fan's Guide*, Black Dog & Leventhal Publishers, 2011.

Lewisohn, Mark. *The Beatles Live – the Ultimate Reference Book*, Pavilion, 1986.

Lewisohn, Mark. *The Beatles Live!* Pavilion, 1986.

Lewisohn, Mark. *The Beatles London*, Hamlin, 1994.

Lewisohn, Mark. *The Beatles Recording Session,* Harmony, N.Y., 1990.

Lewisohn, Mark. *The Beatles: 25 Years in the Life,* Sidgwick & Jackson, 1987.

Lewisohn, Mark. *The Complete Beatles Chronicle*, Harmony Books, N.Y., 1992.

Lewisohn, Mark. *The Complete Beatles Chronicle,* Pyramid Books, 1992.

Lewisohn, Mark. *The Complete Beatles Recording Sessions: The Official Story of the Abbey Road years 1962-1970*, Harmony Books, 1988.

Lewisohn, Mark. *The Beatles - All These Years: Volume One: Tune In*, Little, Brown Book Group, 2015.

Life (ed.). *The Beatles from Yesterday to Today*, Bulfinch, 1996.

Liljedahl, Karen. *The Beatles,* Ariel Books, 2001.

Luppola, L., Durazzi, A. *The Beatles: Italian Tour,* De Ferrari, 2005.

Luppola, Luigi. *The Beatles: Love Me Do,* BFC Pepperland, 2002.

MacDonald, Ian. *Revolution in the Head: The Beatles Records and the Sixties*, Fourth Estate, 1994.

MacDonald, Ian. *The Beatles: L'opera completa*, Mondadori, 1994.

MacIlwain, John. *The Beatles*, Pitkin Guides, 1997.

Mackenzie, Maxwell. *Every Little Thing*, Avon Music/Books, 1998.

Madinger, C., Easter, M. *Eight Arms to Hold You*, 44.1 Productions LP 2000

Madow, S., Sabul, J. *The Colour of Your Dreams: The Beatles Psychedelic Music*, Dorrance Publ. Co., 1992.

Mansfield, Ken. *The Beatles, The Bible and Bodega Bay: A Long and Winding Road*, Permuted Press, 2022.

Mantovina, Dan. *Without You: The Tragic Story of Badfinger*, Francis Glover Books, 1997.

March, I., Greenfield, E., Layton, R. *The Penguin Guide to Compact Discs and Cassettes*, Penguin Books, 1992.

Marion, Larry. *The Lost Beatles Photographs: The Bob Bonis Archive, 1964-1966*, HarperCollins, 2018.

Markworth, Tino. *Bob Dylan and the Beatles: An Introduction*, Hobo Press, 1987.

Marsh, Garry. *The Original Baby: You Can Drive My Car*, Number 9 Books, 1998

Martin G., Hornsby J. *All You Need Is Ears*, MacMillan, 1979.

Martin, G., Pearson, W. *Summer of Love: The Making of Sgt. Pepper*, MacMillan, 1994.

Martin, George. *All You Need Is Ears*, MacMillan, 1979

Martin, George. *The Summer of Love*, Pan McMillan, 1994.

Martin, Marvin. *The Beatles: The Music Was Never the Same*, Franklin Watts, 1996.

Martinez, M., Escudero V. *John Lennon*, Lucar, 1994.

Mason, Paul. *The Maharishi*, Element, 1994.

Matsumoto, Tsuneo. *Beatles' Bootlegs*, Kodansha, 1985.

Matteo, Steve. *Let it Be*, Continuum, 2004.

Maycock, Stephen. *Miller's Rock & Pop Memorabilia*, Reed Books, 1994.

McCabe, Peter. *John Lennon for the Record*, Bantam, 1984.

McCabe, P., Schonfeld, R. D. *Apple to the Core: The Unmaking of the Beatles*, Pocket Books, 1972.

McCartney, Linda. *Light from Within: Photojournals*, Bullfinch Press, 2001.

McCartney, Linda. *Linda McCartney Home Cooking*, Bloosmsbury, 1989.

McCartney, Linda. *Linda McCartney: Plates for '78*, MPL, 1977.

McCartney, Linda. *Linda McCartney's Beste

Vegetarische Gerechten, Kosmos Z&K Uitgevers, 1998.

McCartney, Linda. *Linda's Pictures*, Ballantine, 1976.

McCartney, Linda. *Linda's Summer Kitchen*, Little, Brown & Company, 1997.

McCartney, Linda. *Photographs*, MPL, 1982.

McCartney, Linda. *Roadworks*, Little, Brown & Company, 1996.

McCartney, Linda. *Sixties: Portrait of an Era*, Reed Books, 1992.

McCartney, Linda. *Sun Prints*, Barrie & Jenkins, 1988.

McCartney, Linda. *Wide Open*, Bulfinch, 1999.

McCartney, L., Cox, P. *Home Cooking*, Bloomsbury Publishing, 1989.

McCartney, L., Cox, P. *Linda McCartney's Light Lunches*, Bloomsbury Publishing, 1991.

McCartney, L., Cox, P. *Linda McCartney's Main Courses*, Bloomsbury Publishing, 1991.

McCartney, L., Richardson, R. *Linda's Kitchen*, Little, Brown & Company, 1995.

McCartney, Michael. *Mike Mac's White and Blacks*, Aurum Press, 1986.

McCartney, Mike, *MML Mike McCartney's Liverpool Life*, Garlic Press Publ., 2003.

McCartney, Mike. *Thank U Very Much: Mike McCartney Family Album*, Weidenfeld & Nicholson, 1981.

McCartney, Mike. *Sonny Joe and the Ringdom Rhymes*, HarperCollins, 1992.

McCartney, Paul. *Blackbird Singing: Poems and Lyrics 1965-1999*, Faber and Faber, 2001.

McCartney, Paul. *Give My Regards to Broad Street*, Pavilion, 1984.

McCartney, Paul. *Paintings*, Bulfinsch Press Book, 2000.

McCartney, Paul. *Paul McCartney Composer/Artist*, Pavilion, 1981.

McCartney, Paul. *The Lyrics: 1956 to the Present*, Penguin Books, 2021.

McCartney, Paul. *The Paul McCartney World Tour*, Private Edition, 1990.

McCoy, W., McGeary, M. *Every Little Thing*, Popular Culture, 1990.

McDonald, E., Powers A. *Rock She Wrote*, Plexus, 1995.

McGee Garry, *Band on the Run*, Taylor Trade Publishing, 2000.

McKeen, William. *The Beatles: A Bio-Bibliography*, Greenwood Press, 1989.

McKen, William. *The Beatles*, Greenwood Press, 1972.

McKinney, Devin. *Magic Circles: The Beatles in Dream and History*, Harvard University Press, 2004.

McWilliams, Courtney. *Beatlemania: A Collector's Guide*, Schiffer Book for Collectors, 1998.

McWilliams, Courtney. *Beatles, Yesterday & Tomorrow: A Collectors Guide to Beatles Memorabilia*, A Schiffer Book for Collectors, 1999.

Mellers, Wilfrid. *Twilight of the Gods*, Schirmer/MacMillan, 1973.

Melly, George, *Revolt into Style: The Pop Arts*, Oxford University Press, 1989.

Mendelsohn, John. *Paul McCartney*, Sire, 1977.

Merle, Pierre. *L'Assassinat de John Lennon*, Fleuve Noir, 1993.

Merle P., Volcouve, J. *Les Beatles*, Éditions Solar, 1987.

Miles, Barry. *Paul McCartney: Many Years From Now*, Secker and Warburg, 1997.

Miles, Barry. *The Beatles: A Diary*, Omnibus Press, 1998.

Miles, Barry. *The Beatles: A Diary: Volume 1*, Omnibus Press, 2001.

Mills H., Cockerill, P. *A Single Step: A Memoir*, Warner Books, 2002.

Mitchell, C., Munn, M. *All Our Loving: A Beatles Fan's Memoire*, Robson Books, 1999.

Molnar, I., & G. *Halhatatlan Beatles*, Budapest, 1986.

Moore, Allan F., *The Beatles: Sgt. Pepper's Lonely Hearts Club Band*, Cambridge Music Handbooks, 1997.

Moreton, Jackson David. *The Beatles in Reverse*, Cathmort Books, 2000.

MPL Communications. *Wingspan: Paul*

McCartney's Band on the Run, Little Brown, 2002.

Mulford, Phil. *Bassline: The Beatles*, Wise Books, 1992.

Mulhern, Tom. *Bass Heroes: Styles, Stories & Secrets of 30 Great Bass Players*, GPI Books, 1993.

Munroe, A., Altshuler, B., Hendricks, J. *Yes Yoko Ono*, Japan Society & Harry N Abrams, 2000.

Nagano, M., Shimamoto, S., Spector, D. *Japan Through John Lennon's Eyes*, Shogakukan, 1990.

Neaverson, Bob. *The Beatles Movies*, Cassell Wellington House, 1997.

Neill, Andrew. *Working Class Legend: John Lennon*, UFO Music, 1997.

Neill, Andrew. *The Beatles – Baby It's You: A Visual Record*, Vinyl Experience, 1995.

Neises, Charles P. *The Beatles Reader: A Selection…*, Pierian Press, 1984.

Nesseth, Hans Petter. *A Complete Discography of Norwegian Beatles Records*, Nesseth, 1977.

Newkirk, Ingrid. *Save the Animals: 11 Easy Things You Can Do*, Angus & Robertson, 1991.

Nicolas, *Beatles and Lennon Marmalade and Dynamite*, Ediciones Casser Sl., 1992.

Nishimura, Yoshihisa. *Let's Enjoy the Beatles*, Asuka AV Communications, 1987.

Norman, Philip. *Days in the Life: John Lennon Remembered*. Century, 1990.

Norman, Philip. *Paul McCartney: The Biography*, Orion Publishing Co., 2017.

Norman, Philip. *Shout!: The True Story of the Beatles*, Pan Macmillan, 2004.

Nowlin Harrison, Thomas. *Tall Tales of the Beatles*, Lulu.com, 2005.

O'Bootleg, Dr. Winston. *Hinter Verschlossenen Turen Ein Buch Uber Bootlegs*, Private Publication.

O'Brien, Karen. *Hymn to Her: Women Musicians Talk*, Vigaro Press, 1995.

O'Brien, Ray. *There Are Places I'll Remember*, Ray O'Brien. 2001.

O'Dell, D., Neaverson, B. *At the Apple's Core: The Beatles from the Inside*, Peter Owen, 2002.

O'Donnell, Jim. *The Day John Met Paul*, Hall of Fame Books, 1994.

O'Grady, Terence. *The Beatles: A Musical Evolution*, Twayne, 1983.

Ono, Yoko. *Have You Seen the Horizon Lately?* Museum of Modern Art, 1997.

Ono, Yoko. *Have You Seen the Horizon Lately?* Museum Villa Stuck, 1998.

Ono, Yoko. *Japan Through John Lennon's Eyes*, Cadence Books, 1992.

Ono, Yoko. *Yoko Ono: The Blue Room Event*, Shashin Kagaku Co., 1996.

Orton, Joe. *Head to Toe and Up Against It*, Da Capo Press, 1998.

Palm, Carl Magnus. *Beatles-Beatles*, Tiden, 1996.

Pang, May. *Loving John: The Untold Story*, Warner Books, 1983.

Pang, M., Edwards, H., *John Lennon: The Lost Weekend*, S.P.I. Books, 1992.

Paoli, Gabriele. *Beatles*, Arcana, 1984.

Paoli, Gabriele. *John Lennon*, Arcana, 1984.

Parker A., Bowles, D., Bateson, K. *In the Lap of the Gods and the Hands of the Beatles*, Archway Publishing Company.

Pascall, Jeremy. *Paul McCartney & Wings*, Hamlyn, 1977.

Passian, Rudolf. *Licht Und Schatten Der Esoterik*, Knaur, 1991.

Pastonesi, Marco. *Beatles*, Gammalibri, 1980.

Patterson, James. *The Last Days of John Lennon*, Cornerstone, 2021.

Patterson, R. Gary. *The Walrus Was Paul*, Excursion Prod/Publ., 1994.

Patterson, R. Gary. *The Walrus Was Paul: The Great Beatle Death Clues of 1969*, Dowling Press, 1996.

Patti, D., Holmes, M. *Animal Magnetism*, Smithmark, 1998.

Pawlowski, Gareth L. *How They Became The Beatles*, E.D. Dutton/Penguin, 1989.

Peel, Ian. *The Unknown Paul McCartney*, Reynolds & Hearn, 2002.

Peglau, Andreas. *Alles Was Du Brauchst Ist Liebe*, Zentralhaus Publikation, 1987.

Perry, Harriet L. *Paul McCartney Standing Stone Premiere*, Tracks, 1998.

Pinheiro de Almeida, L., Lage, T. *Beatles Em Portugal*, Assirio & Alvim, 2002.

Pokora, Hans, *Rare Record Cover Book*, Hans Pokora, 1996.

Polidoro, Massimo. *Beatles in Italia*, Beatles Staf Org., 1987.

Pollard, J-L., Jouffa, F. *Le Dictionaire des Beatles*, Michel Lafon, 1995.

Ponomarenko, A., Kozlov, N. *The Beatles: An Encyclopedic Reference Book*, Bibliopolis Publishing House, 1996.

Porter, Richard. *Guide to the Beatles' London*, Abbey Road Cafè, 2000.

Porter, Richard. *Guide to the Beatles' London*, Falkland Press, 2000.

Pritchard, D., Lysaght A. *The Beatles: An Oral History*, Hyperion, 1998.

Quantick, David. *Revolution: The Making of the Beatles' White Album*, Unanimous, 2002.

Ral, J., Bijnens, J. *Beatles in Belgium*, Privately Published, 1996.

Rankin, Robert. *Sex and Drugs and Sausage Rolls,* Transworld Publishers, 1999.

Rayl, A. J. S. *Beatles '64: A Hard Day's Night in America*, Sidgwick & Jackson, 1989.

Reed, John. *I Beatles*, Gammalibri, 1987.

Reeve, Andru J. *Turn Me on Dead Man: The Complete Story of the Paul McCartney Death Hoax*, Popular Culture, 1994.

Rehwagen, Thomas. *Gimme Some Truth*, Pendragon, 1990.

Rehwagen, T., Schmidt, T. *Mach Schau! Die Beatles In Hamburg*, EinfallsReich, 1992.

Reilly, E., McManus, M., Chadwick B. *The Monkees: A Manufactured Image*, Ann Arbor, 1987.

Reinhart, Charles. *The Book of Beatles Lists*, Contemporary Books, 1985.

Reinhart, Charles. *You Can't Do That*, Pierian Press, 1981.

Renwick, Bruce. *The Beatles in New Zealand*, B. Tell Publications, 1993.

Revilla, Jorge L. *The Beatles: 35th Issue in the Series of Rock Images*, La Mascara, 1994.

Rex Features Ltd., Magnus D. *All You Need Is Love: The Beatles Dress Rehearsal*, Tracks, 1997.

Riley, Tim. *Tell Me Why...*, Alfred A. Knopf, 1988.

Riley, Tim. *Tell Me Why...*, Vintage Books, 1989.

Rizzi, Cesare. *Atlanti Musicali Giunti: Beatles*, Giunti, 2002.

Roberts, Jeremy. *The Beatles Biography*, Lerner Publishing Group, 2002.

Robertson, John. *Lennon*, Omnibus Press, 1995.

Robertson, John. *The Art and Music of John Lennon*, Omnibus Press, 1990.

Robertson, John. *The Complete Guide to the Music of the Beatles*, Omnibus Press, 1994.

Rogan, Johnny. *Starmakers & Svengalis*, Futura/MacDonald, 1988.

Rogan, Johnny. *The Complete Guide to the Music of John Lennon*, Omnibus Press, 1997.

Rolling Stone (ed.). *Harrison*, Simon & Schuster, 2002.

Rolling Stone. *The Beatles*, Rolling Stone Press, 1980.

Rolling Stone (ed.). *The Ballad of John and Yoko*, Rolling Stone Press, 1982.

Rorem, Ned. *The Music of the Beatles*, N.Y.R. of B., 1968.

Rowley, David. *Beatles for Sale: The Musical Secrets of the Greatest Rock'n' Roll Band of all Time*, Mainstream Publishing Co.; 2002.

Ruhlman, William. *John Lennon*, Brompton Books/Smithmark, 1993.

Russell, J.P. *The Beatles for the Record*, Scribner's, 1982.

Russell, Jeff. *The Beatles Album File and Complete Discography*, Blandford Press, 1989.

Ryan, M.J. *A Grateful Heart*, Conan Press, 1994.

Rypens, Arnold. *The Originals: In Den Beginne Was Muziek*, De Fontein B.V., 1996.

Saabye, Christensen Lars. *Beatles*, Cappellen, Norway, 1984.

Salewicz, Chris. *McCartney*, St Martins Press, N.Y., 1986.

Salewicz, Chris. *McCartney: The Definitive Biography*, St Martins Pr., 1986.

Saltzman, Paul. *The Beatles: In Rishikesh*, Viking Studio, 2000.

Saltzman, P., Wride, T.B. *The Beatles in India*, Insight Editions, 2018.

Sanmartino, M., Lewi, D., Ravelo, M., Chilabert, R. *A, B, C, D, Paul, John, George Y Ringo!*, Lumiere Ediciones, 2002.

Sanchez, Enrique. *Beatles en el aire: Radionovela de una época*, Editorial Milenio, 1997.

Santrey, Laurence. *John Lennon: Young Rock Star*, Troll Associates, 1990.

Sauceda, James. *Literary Lennon: A Comedy of Letters*, Popular Culture, 1984.

Scaduto, Anthony. *The Beatles*, Signet, 1968.

Schaffner, Nicholas. *The Beatles Forever*, McGraw Hill, 1978.

Schaffner, Nicholas. *The Beatles Forever*, Stackpole Books, 1977.

Schaffner, Nicholas. *The Boys from Liverpool: John, Paul, George, Ringo*, Methuen, 1980.

Scharoff, Mitch. *The Beatles: Collecting the Original UK Pressings*, Mitch Scharoff, 1996.

Scheff, David. *Last Interview (All We Were Saying): John Lennon & Yoko Ono*, Sidgwick & Jackson, 2000.

Scheff, David. *The Playboy Interview with John Lennon & Yoko Ono*, Playboy Press, USA, 1981.

Schmidt, Thorsten. *Gunter Zint – Portrait of Music*, Kultur Buch Bremen, 1998.

Schmidt, Thorsten., *Schwarze Seiten '96*, Kultur Buch, Bremen, 1996.

Schmidt, Thorsten. *Schwarze Seiten '98*, Kultur Buch, Bremen, 1998.

Schmidt, Thorsten. *Schwarze Seiten '99*, Kultur Buch, Bremen, 1999.

Schoeler, H., Schmidt T. *The Beatles Mixes Updated*, Kultur Buch Bremen, 2000.

Schoeler, H., Schmidt T. *The Beatles Mixes*, Kultur Buch Bremen, 1999.

Schreuders P., Lewisohn M., Smith A. *Beatles London*, Hamlyn, 1994.

Schulteiss, Tom. *The Beatles: A Day in the Life*, Pierian Press, 1980.

Schumaker, Susan. Saffel Than, *Vegetarian Walt Disney World and Greater Orlando*, Vegetarian World Guide, 2000.

Schuster, Peter. *Beatles Four Ever: 25 Jahre Beatles*, Beiser Verlag, 1986.

Schuster, Peter. *Four Ever – Die Geschichte Der Beatles*, Belser Verlag, 1989.

Schuster, Peter. *Four Ever: Die Geschichte Der Beatles*, Belser Verlag, 1991.

Schwartz, David. *Listening to the Beatles*, Popular Culture, 1990.

Scwartz, Francie. *Body Count*, Straight Arrow Books, 1972.

Seaman, Frederic. *John Lennon: Living in a Borrowed Time*, Xanadu, 1991.

Seaman, Frederic. *The Last Days of John Lennon*, Dell, 1991.

Searcy, Dawn L. *Warp and Woof! Number 9 Books*, 1990.

Seibold. Jurgen. *Beatlemania VIP*, 1994.

Seibold. Jurgen. *Paul McCartney*, Maewig, 1991.

Seqal, Elaine. *She Loves You*, Simon & Schuster Editions, 1997.

Shapiro, Marc. *Behind Sad Eyes*, St. Martin's Press, 2002.

Shapiro, Mike. *All Things Must Pass*, Virgin Books, 2002.

Shaumberg Ron, *Growing Up with the Beatles*, Pyramid Books, 1976.

Sheff, David. *All We Are Saying: The Last Major Interview with John Lennon and Yoko Ono*, St. Martin's Griffin, 2020.

Sheffield, Rob, *Dreaming the Beatles: The Love Story of One Band and the Whole World*, Dey Street Books, 2018.

Shevey, Sandra. *The Other Side of Lennon*, Sidgwick & Jackson, 1990.

Shinzaki, Kent O. *Can You Dig It?* Cranberry Hill Productions, 1996.

Shinzaki, Kent O. *Clap Your Hands and Stamp Your Feet!* Cranberry Hill Productions, 1998.

Shipton, Paul. *The Beatles*, Pearson Education, 2002.

Shotton, Pete. *John Lennon in My Life*, Stein & Day, 1983.

Sierra I Fabra, Jordi. *Beatles Dictionary*, Plaza & Jones Editores, 1992.

Sierra I Fabra, Jordi. *El Joven Lennon*, Ediciones S.M., 1995.

Sierra I Fabra, Jordi. *The Beatles Diary*, Plaza & Jones Editores, 1995.

Silvester, Christopher. *The Penguin Book of Interviews*, Penguin Books, 1993.

Simpson, Jeff. *Classic Interviews*, BBC Books, 1992.

Smith, Peter. *Two of Us: the Story of a Father, a Son & the Beatles*, Houghton Miffin Co., 2004.

Smith, Joe. *Off the Record*, Sidgwick & Jackson, 1989.

Smout, Michael. *Mersey Stars – An A to Z of Entertainers*, Sigma Press, 2000.

Soffritti, Daniele. *I Beatles dal mito alla storia*, Savelli, Rome, 1980.

Solt, A.. Egan S. *Imagine: The Book*, Bloomsbury Publishing, 1988.

Somach, Danny. *Ticket to Ride*, MacDonald and C., 1989.

Somach, D.. Sharp K. *Meet the Beatles... Again!* Musicom Int., 1995.

Somach, D., Somach K., Muni S. *Ticket to Ride*, MacDonald Books, 1989.

Southall, Brian. *Abbey Road*, Patrick Stephen, 1982.

Southall, B., Vince P., Rouse A. *Abbey Road*, Omnibus Press, 1997.

Southall, Brian. *Beatles Memorabilia: The Julian Lennon Collection*, Carlton Books Ltd, 2013.

Southern, Terry. *Candy & Magic Christian*, Bloomsbury Publishing, 1997.

Spector, R., Waldron V. *Be My Baby*, MacMillan, 1991.

Spencer, Helen. *The Beatles Forever*, Coloro Library, 1982.

Spencer, Terrence. *It was Thirty Years Ago Today*, Bloomsbury Publishing, 1994.

Spignesi, Stephen J. *She Came in Through the Kitchen Window*, Citadel Press, 2000.

Spignesi, Stephen J. *The Beatles Book of Lists*, Citadel Press, 1998.

Spitz, Bob. *The Beatles: The Biography*, Little, Brown & Company, 2006.

Spizer, Bruce. *Fabulous Beatles Records on Vee-Jay*, 498 Productions, 1998.

Spizer, Bruce. *The Beatles on Apple Records*, 498 Productions, 2003.

Spizer, Bruce. *The Beatles Story on Capitol Records: Part 1*, 498 Productions, 2000.

Spizer, Bruce. *The Beatles Story on Capitol Records: Part 2 The Albums*, 498 Productions, 2000.

Stannard, Neville. *The Long and Winding Road*, Virgin Books, 1982.

Stannard, N., Tobler J. *The Beatles: Working Class Heroes*, Avon Books, 1984.

Stern, M., Crawford B., Lamon H. *The Beatles: A Reference & Value Guide Collector Books*, 1993.

Stockdale, Tom. *They Died Too Young: John Lennon*, Parragon, 1995.

Stokes, Geoffrey. *The Beatles*, Rolling Stone Press, 1980.

Stokes, Geoffrey. *The Beatles*, Times Books, 1980.

Sullivan, Henry W. *The Beatles with Lacan*, Peter Lang, 1995.

Sulpy, Doug. *Illegal Beatles: Archival Back Issues 1986-1988*, Storyteller Productions, 1991.

Sulpy, Doug. *The 910's Guide to the Beatles' Outtakes*, the 910, 1996.

Sulpy, Doug. *The 910's Guide to the Beatles' Outtakes*, the 910, 2000

Sulpy, D.. Schweighardt R. *Drugs, Divorce and a Slipping Image*, the 910, 1994.

Sulpy, D.. Schweighardt R. *Get Back: The Beatles' Let It Be Disaster*, Helter Skelter, 1999.

Sulpy, D., Schweighardt, R., *Get Back: The*

Unauthorized Chronicle of the Beatles Let It Be Disaster, St. Martin's Press, 1997.

Sutcliffe, P., Thompson, D. *The Beatles' Shadow*, Sidgwick & Jackson, 2001.

Taormina, Antonio. *I Beatles: Tutti i testi 1962/1970*, Arcana, 1992.

Taormina, Antonio. *John Lennon: Vivendo Cantando Racconti*, Arcana, 1990.

Tarazona, J., Gil R. *George Harrison El Hombre Invisible*, Editorial Milenio, 1999.

Tashian, Barry. *A Ticket to Ride*, Dowling Press, 1997.

Taylor, Alistair. *Yesterday: The Beatles Remembered*, Sidwick & Jackson, 1988.

Taylor, Alistair. *With the Beatles*, John Blake Publishing Ltd, 2011.

Taylor, Derek. *20 Years Adrift*, Genesis Publ., 1984.

Taylor, Derek. *As Time Goes By*, Davis, 1973.

Taylor, Derek. *As Time Goes By*, Sphere Books, 1974.

Taylor, Derek. *It Was 20 Years Ago Today*, Fireside, 1987.

Taylor, J., Taylor D. *Getting Sober... and Loving It!*, Vermillion, 1992.

Taylor, John Alvarez. *Stars, Mythen & Legenden*, Lechner Verlag, 1992.

Terry, Carol D., *Here, There and Everywhere*, Pierian Press, 1985.

the Walrus (ed.), *Beatle People: In Words and Pictures*, Walrus Books, 1987.

Thielow, Edmund. *37 Jahre Beatmusik: The Lords*, Sgt. Pepper Club, 1996.

Thielow, Edmund. *Beatlesmania: Made in the Deutsche Demokratische Republik*, Sgt. Pepper Club, 1996.

Thomson, Elizabeth. *The Lennon Companion: 25 Years of Comment*, MacMillan, 1987.

Thomson, Elizabeth. *The Lennon Companion*, McMillan, 1987.

Thomson, E., Gutman D. *The Lennon Companion*, Da Capo Press. 2004.

Thompson, Phil. *The Best of Cellars*, Bluecoat Press, 1994.

Tillekens, Ger. *Het Geluid Van the Beatles*, Het Spinthuis, 1998.

Todd, Michael. *Beatles for Sale*, AMV Entertainment, 1993.

Toropov, Brandon. *Who Was Eleanor Rigby*, Harper Perennial, 1997.

Tougas, Joe. *The Beatles*, Capstone Press, 2015.

Treacher, Peter. *Strawberry Fields*, Penguin Books, 1989.

Tremlett, George. *The Paul McCartney Story*, Future, 1975.

Trumpler, Stefan. *Title Collaborations*, Editions Benteli Berne, 1997.

Tunzi, Joseph A., *Beatles '65*, JAT Publishing, 2002.

Turner, Michael. *It Won't Be Long: the Beatles in Oldham and Middleton*, Marjensar Productions, 1998.

Turner, Steve. *A Hard Day's Write*, Carlton/Little Brown Books, 1994.

Uller, K., Stormo R., *The Beatles I Norge*, Norwegian Wood, 1994.

Ullrich, Corinne. *Paul Ist Schuld*, Phantom Verlag, 1989.

Uriel, Yarden, *The Beatles: The Way Up*, Yarden Uriel, 1996.

Valic, Miljenko & Friends. *First Complete Catalogue of Licensed Singles*, Gipa Art, 1995.

Van Den Berg, Rob. *Paul McCartney: Solo 1970-1990*, Loeb, 1989.

Van Driver, Lavinia. *The 1975 John Lennon Interview*, Donkey Productions, 1984.

Van Driver, Lavinia. *The Collected Paul McCartney Interviews: Part 1*, Donkey Productions, 1984.

Van Driver, Lavinia. *The Collected Ringo Starr Interviews*, Donkey Productions, 1985.

Van Gelder, Henk. Ligtenberg Lucas, *The Beatles in Holland*, Loeb Uitgevers, 1989.

Van Meekren, Jaap. *Herrineringen En Interviews*, De Prom, 1998.

Varobieva, T., *Istoria Ansamblia "Bitls"*, Musyka, Leningrad, 1990.

Vaughan, Ivan. *Ivan: Living with Parkinson's Disease*, MacMillan, 1986.

Venezia, Mike. *The Beatles, Getting to Know*

the World's Greatest Composers, Children' Press, 1997.

Verlant, G., Perrin, J-É. La scandaleuse histoire du rock, Éditions Gründ, 2012.

Vermeer, Evert. Get Back: 25 Jaar Beatles-Muziek, De Konig Boekproducties, 1988.

Vermeer, Evert. The Beatles: Een Twintigste Eeuwse Legende? AO Actuele Onderwerpen, 1987.

Vlastuin, Frans. De Waterdans, Tournesol, 2002.

Voigts, Andreas. Voigts New Collectors Price Guide for Bootlegs, Indigo Verlag, 1991.

Volcouve, Jacques. Les Beatles, Solar, 1992.

Volcouve, J., Dubreuil M., McCartney, Ergho Press, 1990.

Volcouve, J., Merle, P. Revolution Les Beatles, Fayard, 1998.

Walker, Richard. The Savile Row Story, Prion Multimedia Books, 1988.

Wallgreen, Mark. The Beatles on Record, Simon & Schuster, 1982.

Wane, P., Cornthwaite J., Nash P. Paul McCartney Pics and History, Tracks, 2001.

Warren, Lipack Richard. Epoch Moments and Secrets, Barrister Publishers, 1996.

Welch, Chris. Paul McCartney: The Definitive Biography, Proteus Books, 1984.

Wenner, Jann. Lennon Remembers, Popular Library, 1971.

Whitaker, B., Harrison, M. The Unseen Beatles, HarperCollins, 1991.

White, Charles. The Life and Times of Little Richard, Harmony Books, 1984.

Wiener, Allen J. The Ultimate Recording Guide, Bob Adams, 1994.

Wiener, Jon. Come Together: John Lennon in His Time, Random House, 1984.

Wiener, Jon. Gimme Some Truth: the John Lennon FBI Files, Univ. of California Press, 1999.

Wijnne, Gerrit. Paul McCartney 1942-1966, AO BV, 1999.

Wilk, Max. The Beatles: The Art of the Yellow Submarine, Vinyl Experience, 1994.

Wilk, M., Minoff, L. Yellow Submarine, New English Lib., 1968.

Williams, Alan. The Man Who Gave the Beatles Away, Coronet, 1975.

Willis-Pitts, P. Liverpool, the 5th Beatle: An African-American Odyssey, Amozen Press, 2000.

Wills, Dominic. The Little Book of the Beatles, Carlton Books, 2003.

Wlaschek, M., Pez W. Here, There (and Everywhere?), Modern Music, 1983.

Woffinden, Bob. The Beatles Apart, Proteus Books, 1981.

Wolfgang, S., Van Velsen N. Paul McCartney Paintings, Kultur Verlag, 1999.

Womack, Kenneth. Solid State: The Story of "Abbey Road" and the End of the Beatles, Cornell University Press, 2019.

Woodall, James. Legendarische Liefdes: John Lennon en Yoko Ono, Elmar BV, 1998.

Woog, Adam. The Importance of the Beatles, Lucent Books, 1998.

Wootton, Richard. John Lennon: An Illustrated Biography, Hodder & Stoughton.

Wright, David K. John Lennon, the Beatles and Beyond, Enslow Publishers, 1996.

Yayincilik, Oyko. The Beatles, 1987.

Yenne, Bill. The Beatles, Magna Books, 1989.

Yule, A., McCartney, P. The Man Who Framed the Beatles: A Biography of Richard Lester, Penguin, 1994

Zanetti, Franco. Paul McCartney, Targa Italiana ed., Milan, 1988.

Zint, G., Kruger, U. BIG (Beatles in Germany), Genesis Publications, 1997.

John Mayall on World Tour: This is the first detailed Biography

Dinu Logoz

JOHN MAYALL
THE BLUES CRUSADER

His Life – His Music – His Bands

Englische Originalausgabe /
Original English edition.
304 pp with over 100 pictures in color and b/w
Hardcover 15 × 23 cm
ISBN 978-3-283-01228-1

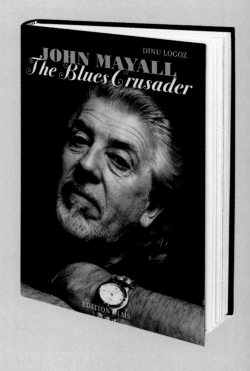

➤ JOHN MAYALL is an icon in the world of blues music and the Godfather of British blues. A pioneering musician, blues promoter and talent scout for over 50 years, his uncanny knack of picking young, talented musicians and then nurturing them in his bands is the stuff of legend. Many young members became huge stars later on, among them brilliant musicians such as Eric Clapton, Peter Green, Jack Bruce, Mick Fleetwood, John McVie, Mick Taylor and drummer Jon Hiseman. In Mayall's bands, an incredible 130 musicians have done their apprenticeship and earned their spurs. Top bands like Cream, Fleetwood Mac or Colosseum would never have existed without his inspiration and guidance.

➤ Now 90 and showing no signs of slowing down, JOHN MAYALL has an amazing back catalogue totalling some 86 albums, and has played over 5000 live concerts all over the world.

➤ This is the first detailed biography of Mayall, illuminating not only his life and career, but also providing deeper, more detailed insights into the development of his many fellow musicians. It follows the young Mayall from the early days of jamming in his tree house as a teenager to the vast tours he undertakes today. Even die-hard blues fans will find a lot of undiscovered anecdotes and stories here, as the book covers all phases of the Mayall's career and not just the 60s.

Table of Contents

RINGO STARR – The definitive Biography of a rock legend!

Nicola Bardola

RINGO STARR

Die Biographie

288 pp with many pictures, Discography and Filmography
Hardcover 15,5 × 23 cm
ISBN 978-3-283-01295-3

➡ **The definitive biography of rock legend Ringo Starr:** Ringo is considered by many rock fans to be the greatest drummer in rock history. With his timing and his unique fills, he gave the Beatles the beat, his beat drove John, Paul and George. In songs such as *Don't Pass Me By, What Goes On, Octopus's Garden* or *With A Little Help From My Friends*, he thrilled a global audience with his unmistakable voice. With his All-Starr Band, Ringo Starr still brings concert halls on every continent to boiling point. And yet Ringo's life is by far the least known of the Fab Four.

➡ Ringo's career before and after the Beatles receives just as much attention here as his time as drummer in the world's most famous rock band. "Peace and love" are probably his most frequently uttered words in this millennium, with his fingers spread out in a peace sign. But what lies behind Ringo's relaxed grin? And where does his persistent longing for peace come from?

➡ This is the world's first comprehensive biography of Ringo Starr, including an interview with Ringo (tbc), discography and filmography. The complete overview for the eightieth birthday on 7 July 2020 of the funniest but most unknown Beatle and eight-time grandfather.

⊞ EDITION OLMS ZÜRICH

Edition Olms AG
Rosengartenstr. 10a
CH-8608 Bubikon/Zürich
Switzerland

Tel. +41(0)43/8449777
Fax +41(0)43/8449778
info@edition-olms.com
www.edition-olms.com